Cambridge Papers in Sociology No. 4

COMMUNITY AND OCCUPATION

COMMUNITY AND OCCUPATION
An exploration of
work/leisure relationships

GRAEME SALAMAN

Lecturer in Sociology, Faculty of Social Sciences
The Open University

Cambridge University Press

Published by the Syndics of the Cambridge University Press
Bentley House, 200 Euston Road, London NW1 2DB
American Branch: 32 East 57th Street, New York, N.Y. 10022

Library of Congress Catalogue Card Number: 73-92781

ISBNs: 0 521 20245 0 *hard covers*
       0 521 09852 1 *paperback*

First published 1974

Set in cold type by EWC Wilkins Ltd, London, and printed in Great
Britain by Alden & Mowbray Ltd, The Alden Press, Oxford

Contents

Preface

My most outstanding debt of gratitude is to John Goldthorpe, who acted as supervisor to the research upon which this book is based. His patient and rigorous criticisms were of enormous value at all times. I am also grateful to Professor Ilya Neustadt and Professor Percy Cohen for their early encouragement, and my colleagues Jeremy Tunstall and Ken Thompson for their suggestions and support. I would also like to thank Kathy Tyrell for her enthusiastic, conscientious and efficient work in preparing the typescript. Bob Blackburn was extremely helpful and diligent in editing the book.

TO MY PARENTS

1
Introduction
Some themes and issues from the classics: the theoretical background

My interest in occupational communities falls within the main-stream of sociological theory and enquiry and has a respectable sociological pedigree. In this introductory chapter some of the themes, issues and problems of the early sociologists that were relevant in the research will be discussed. It would be grossly presumptuous to suggest that these issues and themes are more than connecting threads; certainly there was no intention of testing, clarifying or operationalising them. Quite simply, my interest in occupational communities derived from my earlier interest in these broader theoretical issues and ideas.

It has been convincingly argued that the early 'founding fathers' of sociology were reacting to and attempting to describe and explain the processes of social change that were going on around them. Nisbet refers to these as the two great Revolutions: the Industrial Revolution and the French Revolution.[1]

This interest led to a concentration on one — or possibly two — central sociological problems: social order and social control.[2]

One of the most important elements in the approaches of the founding fathers to these problems was the nature of work, the increasing complexity of the division of labour, and their relationship to the form and type of community and group structure and life. These broad areas of interest were of central importance to the early sociologists.

Nisbet has argued that at a time when the old order was thought to be breaking up, sociologists, historians, philosophers and others rediscovered the central notion of community — and its obverse, alienation — which they tried to use to describe the processes of social change that were taking place. Indeed

---

1 Robert Nisbet, *The Sociological Tradition* (London, Heinemann, 1967).
2 See Alan Dawe, 'The Two Sociologies', *British Journal of Sociology*, vol. 21, no. 2, June 1970, pp. 207–18.

he claims that 'The most fundamental and far-reaching of sociology's unit-ideas is community.'[3]

Marx and Alienation

Marx's interest in the nature of work and man's social or group life is mainly revealed in his writings on alienation. By alienation[4] he meant the separation or estrangement that follows from loss or lack of control and the consequent submission to an external person or system that exploits, and oppresses and is hostile.

Under alienation,

> 'The social character of activity, and the social form of the product, as well as the share of the individual in production, are here opposed to individuals as something alien and material; this does not consist in the behaviour of some to others, but in their subordination to relations that exist independently of them and arise from the collision of indifferent individuals with one another.'[5]

Marx considered that the worker is alienated from his *product* in that it bears no relationship to his needs or creativity, but is merely the result of his supervised production in a system external and hostile to him. The product is hostile in that it is produced for someone else within an economic system that is oppressive and exploitative, *and* because by producing the alienated product within a capitalist system he actually recreates the 'inhuman power' of the system. Marx writes:

> 'But if capital thus appears as the product of labour, the product of labour also appears as capital — no more as a simple product, nor as exchangeable goods, but as capital; objectified labour assumes mastery, has command over living labour . . . the product of labour, objectified labour, has acquired its own soul from living labour and has established itself opposite living labour as an alien force.'[6]

Marx also considered that man is alienated from his *labour*. He did not think that work was necessarily an *inherently* depriving or alienating activity.

3 Nisbet, *The Sociological Tradition,* p. 47.

4 This discussion of Marx and alienation owes a great deal to Richard Schacht's *Alienation* (London, George Allen and Unwin, 1970), and to I. Meszaros' *Marx's Theory of Alienation* (London, Merlin Press, 1970).

5 David McLellan, *Marx's Grundrisse* (London, Macmillan, 1971), p. 66.

6 McLellan, *Marx's Grundrisse,* p. 100.

Indeed, he made it clear that work could be a satisfying and intrinsically delightful activity. Thus, 'Work is a positive, creative activity.'[7] But in capitalist society work *is* alienating, and this alienation involves a number of elements. These are presented in a famous passage:

> 'First, that the work is *external* to the worker, that it is not a part of his nature, that consequently he does not fulful himself in his work but denies himself, has a feeling of misery, not of well-being, does not develop freely a physical and mental energy, but is physically exhausted and mentally debased. The worker therefore feels himself at home only during his leisure, whereas at work he feels homeless. His work is not voluntary but imposed, *forced labour.* It is not the satisfaction of a need, but only a *means* for satisfying other needs. Its alien character is clearly shown by the fact that as soon as there is no physical or other compulsion it is avoided like the plague. Finally, the alienated character of work for the worker appears in the fact that it is not his work but work for someone else, that in work he does not belong to himself but to another person.'[8]

Alienated labour is work done for reasons other than its intrinsic interest and delight; it is work done for someone else — the person who owns and controls the work situation.

The third type of alienation is alienation from other men. It is in the worker's relationships with his colleagues that his alienation is manifested and expressed. Marx anticipated numerous more recent studies in his analysis of the relationship between alienated work and men's inter-relationships. In a society based upon capitalist exploitation alienation is inevitable. In consequence men's relationships will be characterised by calculation, selfishness and self-interest.

In fact men's relationships will reflect their situations as workers.

> 'If a man is confronted by himself, he is confronted by the other man. What applies to a man's relation to his work, to the product of his labour and to himself, also holds of a man's relation to the other man, and to the other man's labour and object of labour . . . one man is estranged from the other.'[9]

7 McLellan, *Marx's Grundrisse,* p. 126.

8 Marx, *Economic and Philosophical Manuscripts of 1844,* in T.B. Bottomore and Maximilien Rubel (eds.), *Karl Marx: Selected Writings in Sociology and Social Philosophy* (Harmondsworth, Penguin, 1963), pp. 177–8.

9 Marx, *Economic and Philosophical Manuscripts of 1844* (London, Lawrence and Wishart, 1967), pp. 72–3.

This alienation of man from man involves a lack of co-operation and friendliness and marked, overt rivalry and competitiveness. However, Marx considered that this state of affairs was not an inevitable aspect of capitalist society, for the time would come when workers would develop close, solidary relationships among themselves. This is clearest where he speaks of the conditions under which the proletariat will cease to be a class in itself — an incoherent mass scattered over the country and broken up by mutual competition[10] — and become a class as a community, a class with a self-conscious sharing of interests and true class consciousness — a class for itself.

Finally, Marx saw alienation in terms of man's view of himself and his ability to develop himself, his potential and his vision. This form of alienation has been called 'dehumanisation' and refers to three basic human characteristics: man's individuality, his social relationships and his 'cultivated sensibility'.

It is important, incidentally, in order to do justice to Marx's notion of alienation, to appreciate that he considered it to be a consequence not of the structure or organisation of any particular firm or work place, nor merely of particular types of supervision or control, but of the capitalist system itself and its emphasis on profit making and the institution of private property. 'Private property is thus the product, the result, the necessary consequence of alienated labour, of the external relation of the worker to nature and to himself.'[11]

Obviously there are a number of themes in Marx's analysis of work, alienation and the bases of community that are relevant to our purposes. The first of these, quite simply, is that he was concerned about the meaning of the work experience in an industrial society. Secondly, he was interested in the relationship between the way in which people relate to each other and the work that they do. These constitute two of the central themes of this study.

But a warning, and digression, may be necessary. In an article, Feuer has asserted that the concept of alienation in Marx's writings changed in both meaning and application.[12] The notion of 'career' could equally well apply to the changing uses to which this concept has been put *since* Marx. Few concepts can have been used in so many ways by so many people. It is easy to see why Schacht, after bravely reviewing the numerous ways in which alienation has been employed, heads his final chapter with a quotation from Ogden

10   See K. Marx and F. Engels, 'The Communist Manifesto', in Bottomore and Rubel, *Karl Marx,* p. 192

11   Marx, *Economic and Philosophic Manuscripts,* p. 76.

12   L. Feuer, 'What is Alienation? The Career of a Concept', *New Politics,* vol. 1, No. 3, 1962, pp. 116–34.

and Richards: 'The temptation ... to use (those) words which are most likely to attract attention and excite belief in the importance of one's subject is almost irresistible.'[13] And Schacht explores in some depth the various uses within sociological literature. A number of points emerge. For one thing it is clear that the usual sociological usage is different from Marx's. This difference is twofold. First, Marx considered alienation to be a result of the capitalist system, not of a particular work situation. Secondly, Marx is not simply dealing with feelings. Most industrial sociologists are, however. Indeed for most sociologists alienation now means certain sorts of answers to certain test items. If you tick *a, b* and *c* you are alienated ... the concept is now 'operationalised'. The next question to ask is: Given that we now have 'measures' of this thing called alienation, what is it? And how does it help us increase our understanding of problematic issues? The answer would seem to be that it helps very little.

It is interesting to consider the reasons for the quite remarkable trivialisation of the concept 'alienation' in industrial sociology. It is tempting to postulate that the shift in emphasis that has taken place may not be unconnected with acceptance, by some sociologists, of the values and concerns of industrial society and industrial management. Alienation thus becomes a sort of attitude survey technique, an investigation of workers' morale.

Tönnies

Tönnies' work on Gemeinschaft and Gesellschaft is sufficiently well known and so obviously fundamental to the topic of this book that a lengthy exposition is redundant. However, a brief sketch of the main elements of his view of social development is in order.

According to Tönnies there are two basic types of social relationship or social organisation: the Gemeinschaft and the Gesellschaft. The former is a relationship characterised by harmony and familial relationships, by 'common goods — common evils; common friends — common enemies'.[14] The use of a common tongue reinforces the shared sentiments, values and beliefs that are typical of the Gemeinschaft. And this form of social organisation is bound together by a consensus which 'represents the special social force and sympathy which keeps human beings together as members of a totality'.[15] Gemeinschaft relationships are 'organic' in nature and are of three types: neighbourhood,

C.K. Ogden and I.A. Richards, *The Meaning of Meaning* (London, Routledge and Kegan Paul, 1949). The quotation is from Schacht, *Alienation*, p. 237.

F. Tönnies, *Community and Association* (London, Routledge and Kegan Paul, 1955), p. 57.

Tönnies, *Community and Association*, p. 53.

kinship and friendship. Members of the Gemeinschaft are all involved in a shared common will, the product of their separate and similar volitions. The development of individualism is minimal.

The Gesellschaft type of relationship or social organisation is in marked contrast to the Gemeinschaft.

> 'The theory of the Gesellschaft deals with the artificial construction of an aggregate of human beings which superficially resembles the Gemeinschaft in so far as the individuals peacefully live and dwell together. However, in the Gemeinschaft they remain essentially united in spite of all separating factors, whereas in the Gesellschaft they are essentially separated in spite of all uniting factors.'[16]

In the Gesellschaft individualism is highly developed, and relationships tend to be based on calculation, on exchange rather than on traditional trust and mutual knowledge. In the Gesellschaft 'everybody is by himself and isolated, and there exists a condition of tension against all others'.[17] This form of society is not a natural, organic type like the former; it is artificial, based not on family law and consensus, but on contract. 'In Gesellschaft every person strives for that which is to his own advantage and affirms the action of others only in so far as and as long as they can further his interest.'[18]

In sum, the differences between these two types, community and association, are represented by Tönnies in a famous passage:

> 'There is a contrast between a social order which, being based upon consensus of wills, rests on harmony and is developed and enobled by folkways, mores and religion, and an order which, being based upon a union of rational wills, rests on convention and agreement, is safeguarded by political legislation, and finds its ideological justification in public opinion.'[19]

There is an obvious similarity, frequently remarked upon, between Tönnie typology and Durkheim's subsequent twin concepts: mechanic and organic solidarity. Tönnies saw societies as moving from the earlier, Gemeinschaft

16 Tönnies, *Community and Association*, p. 74.

17 Tönnies, *Community and Association*, p. 74.

18 Tönnies, *Community and Association*, p. 88.

19 Tönnies, *Community and Association*, p. 261.

type, which is clearly closely-related to medieval society, to the Gesellschaft type, which refers to modern society.

Tönnies' interest in and concern for the processes of social change are well within the sociological tradition of concern over the decline of community. As Nisbet has noted, the idea of community was tremendously important to the early sociologists in their attempts to describe and explain the social and intellectual changes they saw going on around them. Nisbet writes:

> 'Through this typology (of Tönnies), the momentous historical transition of nineteenth century society from its largely communal and medieval character to its modern industrialised and politicised form has been taken from the single context of European history in which it arose and made into a more general framework of analysis applicable to analogous transitions in other ages and other areas of the world.'[20]

As one of that group of writers which was particularly and most explicitly concerned with the notion of community, Tönnies is of considerable importance in our discussion.

But our interest doesn't stop there. Tönnies also talked about the nature of work in the two types of society. Gesellschaft society is capitalist society: at one stage he actually talks about 'bourgeois Gesellschaft society'. It involves a drastic change in the nature of the production process and the organisation of labour, as well as changes in the methods and types of exchange. It also involves changes in the meaning that men attach to their work. In place of the old, Gemeinschaft orientation of the craftsman to his craft, who 'gives himself limitlessly to his job without calculation of units of time and compensation',[21] there now arises a calculating — what might be called today an instrumental — approach to work. Work is seen in terms of its production of commodities, not its intrinsic satisfactions. As Tönnies says:

> 'To the latter (Gesellschaft) belongs manufacturing as contrasted with creation; therefore we speak of mechanical work . . . referring to forging plans, machinations, weaving intrigues, or fabrications which are directed to the objective of bringing forth the means, the exclusive determination of which is that of producing the outward effects necessary to attain our desired ends.'[22]

0 Nisbet, *The Sociological Tradition,* p. 71.
1 Nisbet, *The Sociological Tradition,* p. 76.
2 Tönnies, *Community and Association,* p. 17.

However, it is important to note that Tönnies did not see the relationship between changes in forms of social organisation and economic changes in the same way as Marx. On the contrary, he saw the changes in forms of economic organisation and exchange as the *results* of the move from Gemeinschaft to Gesellschaft.

Weber

Weber's contribution to the themes and issues of this discussion comprises two inter-related themes: bureaucracy and rationality. Once again his work is too well known to require a lengthy exposition, but his views on bureaucracy are clearly closely related to discussions of work organisation and organisation structure, and should be noted.

It has become almost a truism that rationality is one of the central themes in Weber's thought and that this concept, which, it has been suggested, can be seen as analogous to Marx's concept of alienation, served him in his description and evaluation of the process of social change.[23] Certainly rationality or rationalisation was a process that Weber saw taking place in many aspects of life: art, music, religion, etc.; and it is an aspect of, or orientation to, social life that he introduces in his typologies of social action and types of authority. Freund has said:

'increasing rationalisation and intellectualisation have had one decisive consequence, on which Weber laid great stress: they have disenchanted the world. With the progress of science and technology, man has stopped believing in magic powers, in spirits and demons; he has lost his sense of prophecy and, above all, his sense of the sacred. Reality has become dreary, flat and utilitarian, leaving a great void in the souls of men which they seek to fill by furious activity and through various devices and substitutes. A prey to precarious relativism to uncertainty and tedious scepticism, they attempt to furnish their souls with the bric-a-brac of religiosity, estheticism, moralism or scientism — in brief, with a sort of pluralist philosophy which extends an indiscriminate welcome to the most heterogeneous maxims from every part of the world. Mysticism becomes mystification, community becomes communitarianism and life is reduced to a series of unrelated experiences.'[24]

23 For a cogent argument to this effect see J. Freund, *The Sociology of Max Weber* (London, Allen Lane, 1968).

24 Freund, *The Sociology of Max Weber,* pp. 23–4.

Weber's own personal comments on rationalisation as a general process are mostly confined to his essay on 'Science as a Vocation'.[25] There he makes two remarks on the meaning of rationalisation. First, although this process is clearly and structurally tied to the development of science (he says it is 'created by science and scientifically orientated to technology'),[26] it does not simply mean the increase in the individual's knowledge and mastery of his environment or the technology that serves them. As he remarks, most people's knowledge of the technology they rely on is what Berger and Luckmann have called recipe knowledge, that is knowledge of how to use it — or how to get someone else to use it — but not of how it works.[27] This latter type of knowledge is not necessary normally because as Weber says, using the example of a streetcar, 'He (the individual) is satisfied that he may "count" on the behaviour of the streetcar, and orients his conduct according to this expectation',[28] in other words he takes its efficient operation for granted. Weber notes that in this respect modern man knows far less about the workings of his technology than does the savage.

If rationality does not mean increased knowledge in this sense, what does it mean? Simply that it is *possible to know;* that 'if one but wished one could learn it at any time'. He continues, and this is the crux of the matter,

> 'Hence, it means that principally there are no mysterious incalculable forces that come into play, but rather that one can, in principle, master all things by calculation. This means that the world is disenchanted. One need no longer have recourse to magical means in order to master or implore the spirits, as did the savage, for whom such mysterious powers existed. Technical means and calculations perform the service.'[29]

For our purposes the most interesting application of rationalisation in Weber's works is his notion of the ideal type of bureaucracy. This view of bureaucracy, which, as Albrow has suggested, is 'the single most important

25 Max Weber, 'Science as a Vocation', in H.H. Gerth and C.W. Mills (eds.), *From Max Weber: Essays in Sociology* (London, Routledge and Kegan Paul, 1961), pp. 129–56.

26 Weber, 'Science as a Vocation', p. 139.

27 In so doing, of course, they are following Alfred Schutz. See P.L. Berger and T. Luckmann, *The Social Construction of Reality* (London, Allen Lane, 1969), pp. 56–7 and on.

28 Weber, 'Science as a Vocation', p. 139.

29 Weber, 'Science as a Vocation', p. 139.

statement on the subject in the social sciences',[30] emphasises the importance of rules and formal procedures and the employment of full-time, trained experts and officials. It is characterised by a high degree of predictability, formality, calculability, impersonality, specialisation and stability.

Weber clearly believed that the bureaucratic organisation was likely to be efficient because of its characteristics, and for this reason was likely to develop. He writes: 'Precision, speed, unambiguity, knowledge of the files, continuity, discretion, unity, strict subordination, reduction of friction and of material and personal costs — these are raised to the optimum point in the strictly bureaucratic administration.'[31]

Weber goes to some trouble to point out that this type of bureaucracy is also highly rational. It is important to analyse what he means by this. It is clear that he does not mean to equate rationality with efficiency. While not denying that Weber considers bureaucracy to be efficient — and in particular more efficient than other forms of organisation — it should be emphasised that he saw a clear conceptual separation between efficiency and rationality. Efficiency refers to the costs of production and hence to the appropriateness of means to ends. Rationality refers to the application of technical or expert rules to cases. This operation Weber considered rational.

As Albrow has convincingly argued, the relationship between rationality and efficiency is best illustrated by considering the methods used to assess efficiency — which are clearly related to efficiency, but are not the same thing. Accountability, calculability, predictability, reliability are all dominant bureaucratic characteristics (they may or may not be efficient). They are achieve through the impersonal application of expert knowledge and technical and procedural rules to cases. These are the characteristics of rationality.

How is this relevant to this discussion? First, Weber saw this rational type of bureaucracy becoming increasingly common. Therefore an increasing number of people would be employed in the role of salaried official or employee. He thought that such employees would be separated from the means of production in the same way as the manual worker. Secondly, he foresaw that this sort of work situation would not be without its problems and difficulties. He considered that the elimination of 'love, hatred, and all purely personal, irrational, and emotional elements which escape calculation'[32] was a defining feature of bureaucracy. Further than this, he saw bureaucracies

30   M. Albrow, *Bureaucracy* (London, Macmillan, 1970), p. 45.

31   Max Weber, 'Bureaucracy', in Gerth and Mills, *From Max Weber,* pp. 196–244, p. 214.

32   Weber, 'Bureaucracy', p. 216.

as not merely 'dehumanising' but as overwhelming in their control over individual members. He writes:

> 'The individual bureaucrat cannot squirm out of the apparatus in which he is harnessed. In contrast to the honorific or avocational "notable", the professional bureaucrat is chained to his activity by his entire materia and ideal existence. In the great majority of cases, he is only a single cog in an ever-moving mechanism which prescribes to him an essentially fixed route of march. The official is entrusted with specialised tasks and normally the mechanism cannot be put into motion or arrested by him, but only from the very top. The individual bureaucrat is thus forged to the community of all the functionaries who are integrated into the mechanism.'[33]

Weber was well aware of the nature and meaning of work in bureaucratic organisations and the relationship between organisational structure and individual attitudes and behaviour, a relationship that has attracted a good deal of attention in recent years and which forms one of the themes in discussions of worker —or manager — work satisfaction.

Durkheim

Durkheim's interest in the relationship between the individual and society, and the nature of society as a fact *sui generis* and the source of morality, religion, consciousness, etc., led him to pay considerable attention to occupational communities. Durkheim was preoccupied with the nature and role of morals and rules, which he saw as the basis of social life. He writes: 'There is no form of social activity which can do without the appropriate moral discipline.'[34]

In his books Durkheim displayed a particular interest in a concept which subsumes his interest in the relationship between the individual and society and the nature of morality: anomie. In his analysis of suicide rates, Durkheim distinguishes three types of suicide: egoistic, altruistic and anomic. Anomic suicides are those that occur when there are industrial or financial crises or other 'disturbances of equilibrium'.

What exactly is anomie? Quite simply it means a condition of normlessness and lack of regulation, of discipline, of restriction on aspirations. A quotation from *Suicide* should clarify Durkheim's use of this concept:

---

33 Weber, 'Bureaucracy', p. 228.

34 Emile Durkheim, *Professional Ethics and Civic Morals*, translated by Cornelia Brookfield (London, Routledge and Kegan Paul, 1957), p. 14.

11

'To achieve any other result, the passions first must be limited. Only then can they be harmonised with the faculties and satisfied. But since the individual has no way of limiting them, this must be done by some force exterior to him. A regulative force must play the same role for moral needs which the organism plays for physical needs. This means that the force can only be moral . . . either directly and as a whole, or through the agency of one of its organs, society alone can play this moderating role; for it is the only moral power superior to the individual, the authority of which he accepts.'[35]

Anomie is a concept which played an important analytic and evaluative role for Durkheim; he uses it in his analysis of the changing bases of societal integration in *The Division of Labour, Suicide* and in his books on *Socialism* and *Professional Ethics*. It is clear that he considered the chronic, endemic anomie which he saw as an intrinsic feature of modern industrial societies as the most serious single malaise of contemporary society. Nowhere is this more clear than in his *Professional Ethics and Civic Morals*.

In this work, published posthumously, Durkheim makes a distinction between two types of regulative rules: those that are general throughout a society and those that are specific to certain positions or callings. As he says, 'there are as many forms of morals as there are different callings'.[36]

He refers to this situation as 'moral particularism' and it reaches, he says, its peak in occupational—professional ethics.

Now these professional ethics or morals are rarely found outside professions — they are particularly rare in industry and trade, and this worries Durkheim, for he believes that

> It is not possible for a social function to exist without moral discipline. Otherwise, nothing remains but individual appetites, and since they are by nature boundless and insatiable, if there is nothing to control them they will not be able to control themselves. And it is precisely due to this fact that the crisis has arisen from which the European societies are now suffering.'[37]

35 Emile Durkheim, *Suicide: A Study in Sociology,* translated by John A. Spaulding and George Simpson, edited with an introduction by George Simpson (New York, Free Press, 1951), pp. 248—9.

36 Durkheim, *Professional Ethics,* p. 5.

37 Durkheim, *Professional Ethics,* pp. 10—11.

This lack of normative regulation within the worlds of industry and commerce results in the ever-increasing rise in aspirations and hopes which cannot, by their very nature, ever be satisfied. This is chronic, extreme anomie. Durkheim's answer to this follows neatly from his analysis. If anomie arises because of the lack of regulation of aspirations within work then it can be reduced through work-based normative systems — occupational corporations or communities. This solution he expounds in *Socialism, The Division of Labour* and *Professional Ethics and Civic Morals.* In *Socialism* he writes:

> 'But then one will ask where, today, are the moral forces capable of establishing, making acceptable and maintaining the necessary discipline? . . . there is one . . . which perhaps, if transformed, could suit our present state. These are the professional groupings, or corporations.'[38]

And so Durkheim is the only one of the theorists discussed here who considered occupational communities directly, although in a rather idiosyncratic manner. Nevertheless his emphasis on the moral or value element involved in occupational groupings, and his realisation that these depend for their strength on the salience of the relationships within the occupational group, are most important from our point of view and will constitute one of the major topics of this discussion.

The Symbolic Interactionists

Another sort of theoretical perspective that is apparent in this work stems from the approach of the symbolic interactionists. This school and their modern successors share the concern of the founding fathers of sociology — the origins and explanation of social order and social control — but focus on co-operative behaviour within interactions rather than on large-scale, institutional or societal analysis. Their approach differs in emphasis from the work of their theoretical predecessors.

The most important figure in symbolic interactionism was G.H. Mead. Mead's views and those of the symbolic interactionists are usefully summarised elsewhere.[39] Briefly, Mead sought to explain co-operative behaviour. Co-operative social behaviour involves actors being able to anticipate each others' reactions and intentions. Mead writes:

38 Emile Durkheim, *Socialism.,* edited and with an introduction by Alvin Gouldner (Collier Books and Antioch Press, New York, 1962), p. 245.

39 Arnold Rose, 'A Systematic Summary of Symbolic Interaction Theory', in Arnold Rose (ed.), *Human Behaviour and Social Processes* (London, Routledge and Kegan Paul, 1971), pp. 3—19.

'The human individual is a self only in so far as he takes the attitude of another toward himself. In so far as this attitude is that of a number of others, and in so far as he can assume the organised attitudes of a number that are co-operating in a common activity, he takes the attitudes of the group toward himself, and in taking this or these attitudes he is defining the object of the group, that which defines and controls the response.'[40]

This is the self, the Me. Co-operative behaviour then follows peoples' ability and propensity to internalise the other and thus react predictably, regularly and reliably through the sharing of symbols, meanings and values. Society is seen as resting on a consensus of agreed expectations, symbols, 'typifications', taken-for-granted regularities and shared knowledge.[41]

Several of the Meadian concepts have been taken up and developed by more recent writers in their investigations of identity-building processes and the management of identities.[42]

From our point of view the important concept is that of the career, which is now used in a wider sense than the purely occupational, to refer to progress through identity-bestowing situations. As such it can be as usefully and legitimately used in analysing the process of *becoming* a madman as of becoming a psychiatrist, of becoming a criminal as of becoming a policeman.

The notion of career, which ties together in a useful way the interactionist concepts of identity, reference group, roles and role expectations (and, by implication, deviance), stresses the way in which selected others are important in supporting one's valued self-image, and includes the idea of career contingencies: factors on which mobility from one position to another depend. As William James pointed out, long before these notions were systematically discussed and expounded: 'it is his image in the eyes of his own "set" which exalts or condemns him as he conforms or not to certain requirements that may not be made of one in another walk of life.'[43]

---

40   G.H. Mead, *The Philosophy of the Present* (Chicago, Open Court Publishing Company, 1932), p. 192.

41   Paul Bohannon has argued convincingly that this conceptual consensus is in fact what Durkheim meant by the conscience collective. See his article: 'Conscience Collective and Culture', in Kurt H. Wolff (ed.), *Essays on Sociology and Philosophy by Emile Durkheim, et al.* (New York, Harper and Row, 1964), pp. 77–96.

42   Most notably by E. Goffman in his *The Presentation of Self in Everyday Life*, (New York, Doubleday, 1959), and *Where the Action Is* (London, Allen Lane, 1969). Strauss' work is also pertinent. See A. Strauss, *Mirrors and Masks* (Glencoe, Illinois, Free Press, 1959).

43   William James, 'The Self', in Chad Gordon and Kenneth J. Gergen (eds.), *The Self in Social Interaction* (New York, Wiley, 1968), pp. 41–9, p. 42.

14

This is exactly the point that the notion of career brings out nicely: that involvement in certain roles is likely to bring one into contact with, and under pressure to accept, a certain perspective incorporating values, attitudes and views — in short, a reference group perspective. This idea of a reference group as a source of values etc. is derived from Shibutani. He says:

'A perspective is an ordered view of one's world — what is taken for granted about the attributes of various objects, events, and human nature. The environment in which men live is an order of things remembered and expected as well as of things actually perceived. It includes assumptions of what is plausible and what is possible.'[44]

The significant others — the reference group — thus assume saliency as the 'set' whose esteem or condemnation is of importance. What is more, those concerned tend to see themselves in terms of their membership of this group, the perspectives it involves, and the titles or labels it carries. They will become, in their own, their peers' and outsiders' eyes, certain sorts of people: homosexuals, jazz men or whatever.[45] This identity has importance either because it is one that they value — because it is the result of lengthy training and carries high status — or because it is one that is highly pervasive and difficult to get away from. Usually it is simply something that stems, unquestioned, from their participation in a particular way of life with particular associates.

This study is concerned with the investigation of this sort of identity-giving process and its relationship to reference group affiliation (and the perspectives that follow), choice of friends and associates.

This then is the theoretical background which culminated in the research reported here. It must, however, be obvious that the ideas and themes mentioned are not sufficient to supply a coherent and systematic approach to the subject of work. For this the work of E.C. Hughes was useful and important.

44 T. Shibutani, 'Reference Groups and Social Control' in Rose, *Human Behaviour*, pp. 128–47.

45 Becker is good on this: 'Members of organised deviant groups have one thing in common: their deviance. It gives them a sense of common fate, of being in the same boat. From a sense of common fate, from having to face the same problems, grows a deviant subculture: a set of perspectives and understandings about what the world is like and how to deal with it, and a set of routine activities based on those perspectives.' (H.S. Becker, *Outsiders* (New York, Free Press, 1963), p. 38.) This process is not restricted to deviants, it also occurs, in a more overt way, in occupational groups.

There are a number of elements and suggestions in Hughes' work —
especially his *Men and Their Work* [46] — which have been used in this analysis.
First is his suggestion, which has of course been taken up by more recent
writers (particularly Becker and other sociologists concerned with professionals) [47]
that 'A man's work is as good a clue as any to the course of his life and his
social being and identity.' [48] This interest leads him to discuss the relationship
between personality types (personality being defined in terms of internalised
attitudes and values), the division of labour, and the ways in which occupations
and their titles are incorporated into men's self-images.

Hughes also makes a lot of the idea of career, which he defines in a rather
different way from the symbolic interactionists, as a subjectively meaningful
account or narrative of one's biography. As such, a career is an actor's attempt
to impose an ordered meaning on the events, identities, interactions, etc., that
he has been exposed to or involved in. Clearly, then, a career will be closely
tied to the various institutional contexts within which he has moved, but
marshalled into a personal, subjectively meaningful coherence.

A second theme is the notion of change and process. This has two aspects:
changes in the structure and nature of occupations and work — through technological or organisational change — and change in the actor's life and psychology
as a result of his progress through a career. Although the study reported later
was not a longitudinal one, it did focus, as will be seen, on these sorts of
changes.

A third theme is the investigation of the way people see their work, how
they evaluate it and its role in society, how they make it meaningful and protect
themselves from possible implications damaging to their identity. This includes
an interest in occupational cultures, in other words the norms and values,
taken-for-granted-knowledge and mutual expectations, the shared work-based
world views, perspectives and rationalisations that occupations sometimes
involve.

Hughes makes further points which are maintained here: that the study of
occupations and work is not an esoteric sub-section of industrial sociology —
nor, still worse, a redundant aspect of organisational theory — but a central
area of sociological investigation that may supply insights and ideas which can
fruitfully be applied in other areas (the work of Hughes himself is an example

46   E.C. Hughes, *Men and Their Work* (Glencoe, Illinois, Free Press), 1958.

47   H.S. Becker and A.L. Strauss, 'Careers, Personality and Adult Socialisation',
     American Journal of Sociology, 1956, pp. 253–63. See also R.K. Merton,
     G.G. Reader and Patricia L. Kendall (eds.), *The Student–Physician* (Harvard
     University Press, 1957).

48   Hughes, *Men and Their Work*, p. 7.

of this); also, that it can be useful to ignore, temporarily, the 'normal' categorisations of occupations (skilled, artistic, professional, criminal, etc.) and treat them together; or to apply findings from work on one to another type of occupation not usually considered similar. Hughes advocates that one should categorise occupations in terms of their *actual* similarities as the sociologist finds them (or as they are seen by those concerned) rather than merely employ the sorts of occupational categories current in the society. In this way one can argue for certain similarities between janitors and doctors, between pool-room hustlers and railwaymen, between prostitutes and professionals.

2
The components and determinants of occupational communities

The subject of this book is work, the meaning of work and the relationship between men's work and non-work lives. As noted in the previous chapter, Hughes' *Men and Their Work* has been most useful as a source of ideas and insights, and the questions he asks early in that book are basic to this enquiry:

> 'To what extent do persons of a given occupation "live together" and develop a culture which has its subjective aspects in the personality? Do persons find an area for the satisfaction of their wishes in the association which they have with their colleagues, competitors, and fellow servants? . . . What part does one's occupation play in giving him his "life organisation"?[1]

It is obvious that the work that men do is likely to have many consequences for the rest of their lives, and the investigation of the ways in which people's non-work lives are affected by various features of their work — its technological organisation, bureaucratic structure, etc. — is an established and well-documented type of sociological enquiry. In particular, much attention has been given to investigating the effects of working in large-scale assembly-line plants.[2] Earlier investigators, particularly those who worked under Hughes, studied the effect of work on men's lives by analysing particular occupational roles and demonstrating their implications for incumbents' non-work lives. Recently other studies have adopted a similar approach.[3]

This book is concerned with exploring and delineating a particular type of work/non-work relationship; a type of relationship which, though it has been well illustrated by many studies, has never been thoroughly analysed and discussed: the occupational community.

1   Hughes, *Men and Their Work,* p. 25.

2   F.H. Blum, *Towards a Democratic Work Process* (New York, Harper and Row, 1953), and R. Blauner, *Alienation and Freedom* (University of Chicago Press, 1964).

3   M. Banton, *The Policeman in the Community* (London, Tavistock Publications, 1964).

Many studies of occupational communities have been carried out, but the data they include vary enormously in quality and type; for rarely is an account of an occupational community the result of an investigation of the community itself. Frequently the community is merely described in rather general, impressionistic terms in the course of some other investigation. Nearly all these studies are accounts of specific communities; they do not attempt to generalise about the nature of the phenomenon *per se.*

An occupational community represents a particular relationship between men's work and the rest of their lives[4] — a type of relationship which in its extreme form is probably increasingly rare in modern societies. Members of occupational communities are affected by their work in such a way that their non-work lives are permeated by their work relationships, interests and values. (Indeed it is likely that members of some communities would not approve of the separation of work and non-work.) Members of occupational communities build their lives on their work; their work-friends are their friends outside work and their leisure interests and activities are work-based. The description Mills gives of the meaning of work to the traditional craftsman can also be applied to members of occupational communities.

> 'In the craftsman pattern there is no split of work and play, of work and culture . . . The craftman's work is the mainspring of the only life he knows; he does not flee from work into a separate sphere of leisure; he brings to his non-working hours the values and qualities developed and employed in his working time. His idle conversation is shop talk; his friends follow the same line of work as he, and share a kinship of feeling and thought.[5]

In this book an attempt will be made, based on a review of many published studies, to list the components and determinants of occupational communities and to suggest a classification of types.[6] It is clear that members of these

4 An occupational community means that people who are members of the same occupation or who work together have some sort of common life together and are, to some extent, separate from the rest of society. The most important element of this separation, and the one that has been employed most often as the defining characteristic of an occupational community, is 'the convergence of informal friendship patterns and colleague relations'. (J.E. Gerstl, 'Determinants of Occupational Community in High Status Occupations', *Sociology Quarterly,* 1961, pp. 37—48.) Not all the studies referred to in this book use this definition of occupational communities — some do not define the phenomenon at all — but all mention that members of the occupation form a separate and distinctive group.

5 C.W. Mills, *White Collar: The American Middle Classes* (New York, Galaxy, 1956), pp. 222—3.

6 There is no advantage at this stage, in defining arbitrary limits to an occupational community. It is probably more useful to talk about degrees of occupational community.

communities present a degree of convergence in work and non-work activities, interests and relationships which is in marked contrast to the work/non-work relationship demonstrated by many other workers. Some workers, indeed, seem to deliberately reject the sort of behaviour displayed by members of occupational communities. In recent years, attention has been drawn to those workers who, as a result of their particular view of the nature of work and the rewards it brings, attempt to enforce a rigid separation of their work and non-work lives. It has been shown that these workers have virtually no interest in their plant as a source of out-of-plant relationships or interests: when they leave it they apparently want to free themselves from anything or anybody that might remind them of what they regard as an unpleasant, depriving experience.[7]

It is therefore very important and interesting to investigate those workers who belong to occupational communities and who, by allowing a fusion of their work and non-work lives, present such a marked contrast with workers who separate the two spheres of life. For some people the occupational group still functions as a basis of association and identification: it is important to discover the circumstances under which this occurs.

The model of the determinants and components presented below was derived from a thorough study of the existing accounts of occupational communities; it is an abstraction of the factors that are mentioned in these accounts.

Before the scheme is presented, an important distinction must be made between the 'quasi' and the 'true' occupational community. 'Quasi' occupational communities, which are excluded from this analysis, are those communities that are the result of a geographically isolated or spatially segregated area or work place, dominated by a single firm or industry. In such a case — where the community is the result of isolation *per se* — the resulting *community-like* patterns of group life *must* develop, willy nilly. Anything which reduces the self-sufficiency of the area will result in the breakdown of the community. This point has been emphasised by Brennan *et al.* He and his co-authors argue that the decline of communities in South West Wales is due to the increased mobility of the inhabitants and their exposure to a national rather than a local culture — both these factors resulting in the reduced self-sufficiency of the area. The authors say: 'Anything which tends to make each community less self-contained and more inclined to "trade" socially with

7   John H. Goldthorpe, David Lockwood, Frank Bechhofer and Jennifer Platt, *The Affluent Worker: Industrial Attitudes and Behaviour* (Cambridge University Press, 1968). See also Chris Argyris, *The Applicability of Organizational Sociology* (Cambridge University Press, 1972).

its neighbouring communities will result in more specialisation of functions between them.'[8]

Such communities will not be dealt with here. Instead emphasis will be placed on distinguishing the components and determinants of occupational communities which are the result of features of members' work and not simply of the geographical isolation of the area.

Of course this distinction will not always be an easy one to enforce. Some 'true' occupational communities — such as those of fishermen or coalminers — sometimes also tend to involve geographical or spatial separation; but it is argued that they would occur without this.

The Components of Occupational Communities

What then are the key, defining components of an occupational community? First, members of occupational communities see themselves in terms of their occupational role: their self-image is centred on their occupational role in such a way that they see themselves as printers, policemen, army officers or whatever, and as people with specific qualities, interests and abilities. Secondly, members of occupational communities share a reference group composed of members of the occupational community. Thirdly, members of occupational communities associate with, and make friends of, other members of their occupation in preference to having friends who are outsiders, and they carry work activities and interests into their non-work lives. Each of these three components will be discussed in turn.

A self-image is the way that a man sees himself. This self-perception is not a random, idiosyncratic affair, but is in terms of certain social roles and is based upon the support and confirmation of certain 'significant others'. The subtle ways in which a person's identity is established and sustained, the mechanisms adopted to ensure recognition and acceptance of one's self-image,[9] the way in which individuals search out those situations which are most likely to confirm their self-images, and the potential anxiety[10] which can be unleashed when a person's self-image is consistently denied, are all issues connected with self-image which have come under sociological analysis. We, however, are particularly interested in the way in which an occupational role can be taken as a primary element in a man's self-image and how this is supported by others who are also incumbents of this role. The idea that an occupational role can

---

8   T. Brennan, E.W. Cooney and H. Pollins, *Social Change in South West Wales* (London, Watts, 1954), pp. 44—5.

9   Goffman, *The Presentation of Self in Everyday Life.*

10 H.H. Gerth and C.W. Mills, *Character and Social Structure* (London, Routledge and Kegan Paul, 1954), pp. 80—125.

become an integral part of a person's self-image is not, of course, by any means original. As Park put it,

> 'The conceptions which men form of themselves seem to depend upon their vocations, and in general upon the role which they seek to play in the communities and social groups in which they live, as well as upon the recognition and status which society accords them in these roles.'[11]

A persons's self-image, which can be defined as 'a set of attitudes, beliefs and opinions held by a person about himself,'[12] depends for its stability and persistence on the support, encouragement, recognition and acceptance of certain others with whom the actor has relationship. When a man's self-image is centred on his occupational role the others will be his occupational colleagues.

At the same time Goffman has suggested that actors might sometimes attempt to *distance* themselves from the identities implicit in certain activities. This is because all individuals play many more than one role and must try and balance all the identities that their role-playing supplies. It is important to remember that, although it is true that people's identities are largely the result of the roles they play, they are not the result of *any one single role,* and that 'the individual limits the degree to which he embraces a situated role, or is required to embrace it, because of society's understanding of him as a multiple-role-performer rather than as a person with a particular role.'[13] Why then are some roles more likely to be embraced than others? Goffman suggests that roles that have implications for off-duty life are especially likely to be the source of identification. Equally it is possible that people are as likely to over-embrace as to distance themselves from the identities inherent in role activity. Such a person might undergo a self-imposed and voluntary course of anticipatory socialisation before entering an occupational role, or display in an extreme, exaggerated form the role requirements, e.g. Merton's bureaucratic virtuoso.

Members of such communities will not only see themselves in terms of their occupational role, they will also value this self-image. This process is unlikely to occur among people who are in occupations that do not have occupational communities, and it is extremely unlikely among those workers who have an

11 R. Park, 'Human Nature, Attitudes and Mores', reprinted in C. Gordon and K.J. Gergen (eds.), *The Self in Social Interaction* (New York, Wiley, 1968), p. 94.

12 William A. Faunce, *Problems of an Industrial Society* (New York, McGraw-Hill, 1968), p. 93. Faunce uses the disjuncture between our evaluation of ourselves and others' evaluation of us as a criterion of alienation.

13 Erving Goffman, 'Role Distance', in *Where the Action Is,* pp. 37–103, p. 94.

'instrumental' orientation towards their work and who wish to escape totally from their work once they leave the work place.

One study of an occupational community which is particularly rich in information on the process described above is Becker's study of jazz musicians. Becker makes it eminently clear that the jazz men he met saw themselves in terms of their occupational role and that this self-image over-shadowed earlier identities. For example, he mentions one man who said that his identity as a jazz musician had meant that he was no longer concerned about other identities that he had once valued, and that although he was Jewish this was no longer a part of his self-image.[14] It is probably to professionals that the notion of an occupational self-image has been most frequently applied. Goode, for instance, has said that one of the characteristics of a profession is that the members share a common identity.[15] But this is true not only of professionals; it also occurs among members of all occupational communities.

People who see themselves in terms of a particular occupational title will do so only when they have satisfied themselves — and others — of their *right* to this title. They will ignore and resist premature labelling by uninitiated outsiders who, being unaware of the subleties involved in the passage from recruit to full member of the occupation, call trainees by the full occupational title when they have not yet earned it. The stages through which a member of an occupation has to pass to attain full membership may be more or less formal and institutionalised. In the case of professionals the stages are not only highly institutionalised (examinations, internship, articles, pupilage, office practice, etc.), but the title often carries legal status.

Becker and Carper have pointed out that when people see themselves in terms of their occupational roles they see themselves as certain sorts of people with particular qualities and capacities, for whom some behaviour is appropriate while some is not. In fact, it means that the people concerned internalise a value system. These investigators remark:

> 'Kinds of work tend to be named, to become well-defined occupations and an important part of a person's work-based identity grows out of his relationship to his occupational title . . . They (the occupational titles) imply a great deal about the characteristics of their bearers and these meanings are often systematised into elaborate ideologies which itemise the qualities, interests, and capabilities of those so identified.'[16]

14 Becker, *Outsiders,* p. 99.

15 W.J. Goode, 'Community within a Community: The Professions', *American Sociological Review,* vol. 22, 1957, pp. 194–200.

16 H.S. Becker and J.W. Carper, 'Elements of Identification with an Occupation', *American Sociological Review,* vol. 21, 1956, pp. 341–8.

Evidence from studies of occupational communities strongly suggests that their members see themselves in terms of their occupational membership and that this involves the internalisation of a value system. Men not only see themselves as printers or policemen or army officers, but are also able to describe the qualities and characteristics of members of these occupations. The value and belief systems which are held by members of occupational communities are frequently relevant not only to the world of work but to many other aspects of members' lives.

Occupational or professional cultures involve values which define the 'real' or proper nature of the work — what scientists or sociologists *ought* to be doing — and the necessary conditions for doing this work (for example Merton's work on the value systems of scientists). Box and Cotgrove have pointed out, of course, that it is not safe to assume that all members of an occupation share the same commitment to the occupational values.[17] An occupational culture also involves beliefs about the nature of the service the occupation supplies to the larger society and the nature of the relationship between members of the occupation, their clients and society. In this sense it involves ideological elements. It also involves assumed knowledge among members of the occupation, knowledge which may be transmitted and referred to through a special *argot*. This *argot* serves, as Polsky has suggested and as the research reported here confirms, to separate the insiders from the outsiders and as a technical language — a way of describing the techniques, processes, methods and tools of the trade.[18] Members of occupational communities live in their own separate world, a mental world composed of assumptions, attitudes, knowledge, expectations and shared history.

One of the most striking facts to emerge from all the studies of occupational communities is that members of these communities share view-points, attitudes and values with other members. Members of occupational communities use the community as a primary reference group. The incorporation of an occupational role into one's self-image is obviously directly related to the use of the occupational community as a reference group, for the values which accompany this identification will be derived from the reference group; and the other members of the reference group will be the 'significant others' whose support is so important in this respect and who are capable of exercising powerful social sanctions.

---

17 R.K. Merton, *Social Theory and Social Structure* (Glencoe, Illinois, Free Press, 1962); Stephen Cotgrove and Steven Box, *Science, Industry and Society* (London, Allen and Unwin, 1970).

18 Ned Polsky, *Hustlers, Beats and Others* (Harmondsworth, Penguin, 1971), pp. 105–14.

There are various ways in which the concept of reference group has been used; it is used here in the normative sense – i.e. a reference group as a source of values, as Shibutani has put it, as a perspective. As a consequence of their shared values, members of occupational communities will tend to see the reactions and responses of their fellow members as being of particular importance, and they will regard their fellow members as the only other people who are really capable of judging their work performance or understanding their problems. One occupational community which reflects this attitude is again that of the jazz musician. Mack and Merriam say: 'It is the judgements of their own group that he (the jazz musician) considers valid, and their terms which shape his life . . . (they) tend to live on their own terms for their own pleasures.'[19]

The idea that members of an occupation might use a reference group based on the occupation has been most frequently applied to professionals, and professionals are notable for the degree to which practitioners share a value system, as a result of which they regard the judgements of their professional colleagues as having special importance. Gouldner says of the professional who works in non-professional organisations:

'his continued standing as a competent professional often cannot be validated by members of his employing organisation, since they are not knowledgeable enough about it. For these reasons, the expert is more likely than others to esteem the good opinion of professional peers elsewhere; he is disposed to seek recognition and acceptance from outsiders.'[20]

Members of occupational communities do not attempt to separate their work and non-work lives: their work influences their non-work activities and interests. Members of such communities manifest a strong convergence of work and non-work life generally, and the most important feature of this is that they prefer to be friends with people who do the same work. This does not simply mean that members of occupational communities are friendly with their work-mates while at work, for other researchers have shown that many groups of workers claim to be 'friendly' with their work-mates while they work together.[21] For members of occupational communities, colleague

19   R.W. Mack and A.P. Merriam, 'The Jazz Community', *Social Forces,* vol. 35, 1960, pp. 211–22, p. 220.

20   H.P. Gouldner, 'Dimensions of Organisational Commitment', *Administrative Science Quarterly,* vol. 4, 1960, pp. 468–90.

21   Goldthorpe *et al., The Affluent Worker;* A.J.M. Sykes, 'Navvies: Their Social Relations', *Sociology,* vol. 3, 1969, pp. 157–73; and S.M. Lipset, M.A. Trow and J.S. Coleman, *Union Democracy: The Internal Politics of the International Typographical Union* (Glencoe, Illinois, Free Press, 1956), pp. 171–5.

relationships permeate out-of-work life. Colleague relationships imply more than just a shared work situation. A colleague is someone who is a member of the same occupation, certainly, but more than this, he is someone who inhabits the same normative and associational world. Colleagueship involves a trust, a confident mutuality. It means sharing the same work-based stock of knowledge and meanings, symbols and, as previously noted, language.[22] Members of occupational communities spend time outside working hours with others who do the same work and members of their occupation tend to predominate among their best friends. This is particularly clear in Lipset's account of the American printers' occupational community. He says that:

> 'The formal community of printers' clubs is paralleled by an informal one. That is, large numbers of printers spend a considerable amount of their leisure time with other printers. In interviews many printers reported that their best friends are other printers, that they regularly visit the homes of other printers, that they often meet in bars, go fishing together, or see each other in various places before and after work.'[23]

Similarly, studies of jazz musicians make much of the fact that members of this occupation are socially isolated from the rest of society and that they restrict their association to within their occupational group.

This convergence of work and non-work relationships is by no means a general tendency; workers in some occupations deliberately avoid any out-of-work friendships or associations with people who work with them or who are in the same occupation, or at any rate they show no particular propensity to associate with them.

It is important at this stage to make a distinction which will be more fully developed later. Members of some occupational communities associate with, and make friends of, people they actually work with; while members of other communities make friends of people who do the same work but who work elsewhere and who do not share their specific work situation. This distinction will be developed later, for it will be argued that it is one of the crucial differences between two different types of occupational community.

Members of occupational communities not only select their friends and associates from among those who do the same work, they also frequently talk about their work outside working time, indulge in work-connected reading, have work-connected hobbies and belong to work-connected societies or clubs.

22   See Polsky, *Hustlers, Beats and Others,* for a description of the functions of colleagueship among hustlers.

23   Lipset *et al., Union Democracy,* p. 70.

Once again it is important to point out that this is by no means true of members of all occupations. Having friends from the same occupation as one-self and spending non-work time in some sort of work-connected activity are obviously closely related phenomena.

When members of an occupation associate with other members, they are associating with people who hold the same values as themselves and who share and support their occupational self-image. The various components of an occupational community are therefore strongly inter-connected.

The Determinants of Occupational Communities

In this section the factors which have been treated, in one form or another, by various writers, as determinants of occupational communities, will be described, and it will be shown how each of the three basic determinants which emerge is related to some or all of the components which were des-cribed in the last section. Later the relative causal importance of these deter-minants will be discussed, for although all are, under certain circumstances, causally related to some or all of the components, one determinant appears to have considerably greater causal importance than the other two.

The determinants relate to three situations and are: involvement in work tasks, marginal status or stratification situation, and the inclusiveness of the work or organisational situation. The determinants have been synthesised from a close survey of the existing literature on occupational communities, and although none of these studies actually mentions all three in anything like this form, they all mention one or more of them in some way or other. Gerstl is the only writer who has attempted a classification of determinants of occupational communities, rather than just an account of the determinants involved in a single case. The determinants he isolates can all be subsumed under the three mentioned above, but the only one which is common to this study and Gerstl's is involvement — which he regards as the most important determinant of occupational communities. However he does not discuss it in any great detail, nor does he specify the *objects* of the involvement.[24]

Members of occupational communities are emotionally involved in their work skills and tasks; they value their work not only for the extrinsic re-wards it brings but also for the satisfaction they derive from actually doing it, and for the opportunities it offers them to use their work skills. This is beautifully demonstrated in the case of poolroom hustlers, who, Polsky tells us, 'live in the poolroom and clearly have a well developed occupational community'. Polsky writes: 'When a hustler says of hustling that "it beats

24   Gerstl, 'Determinants of Occupational Community'.

working" his emphasis is not on putting down the workaday world; his primary meaning is, rather, a positive one — that hustling is infinitely more pleasurable than any other job he could find.'[25]

Members of occupational communities derive intrinsic satisfaction from their work and see it as an activity within which they can exercise creativity, responsibility and intelligence. Men who see their work in this way are likely to carry work-based activities, interests and relationships into their non-work lives; they are not likely to erect a barrier between work and non-work as some workers do. As Gerstl has said: 'The man who finds his work to be merely a means of making money would be less likely to seek out his colleagues in his leisure time than would the man who finds his work to be a constant source of stimulation.'[26]

Although involvement refers to a type of attitude towards work, and is therefore to some extent a result of factors external to any particular work situation, it is probably true that some types of work generate more involvement than others. Certain factors in particular appear to be important. Danger is one. There are a number of accounts of occupational communities which are based upon jobs involving danger: for example deep-sea fishing or coal-mining. Jobs which are considered to be responsible, in the sense that a mistake could mean endangering the public in some way, also seem to arouse considerable involvement on the part of those concerned. Engine drivers are a case in point. The skill level of a job is also an important factor. When a job requires a high level of expertise and skill on the part of its practitioners, they are likely to display a marked degree of involvement in it and to derive satisfaction from the execution of the work tasks. Finally, the status of a job is an important consideration. When a job is accorded high status *vis-à-vis* other local jobs it is likely that its practitioners will be prepared to make a greater personal investment in it. Again railwaymen are an example. Traditionally the railway has been a high-status working-class job, although its relative status position has declined recently.

Of course one would expect to find a high degree of correlation between the determinants of occupational communities — i.e. the reasons why people prefer to associate with their colleagues and carry work activities and interests out of work (or to reject the very notion of the division of the world into work and non-work) — and the components of such occupational communities. People who spend their time with colleagues talking about work-connected matters, etc., are likely to develop orientations and attitudes towards their

25   Polsky, *Hustlers, Beats and Others*, p. 73.

26   Gerstl, 'Determinants of Occupational Community', p. 46.

work that, in turn, cause them to see it as a source of meaningful experience. They are likely *to learn* to value their work activity. Goldthorpe *et al.* have demonstrated the importance of out-of-plant orientation in understanding work attitudes and behaviour.[27] This is as true of men who display a positive orientation as a negative one. But, despite this, men are more likely to involve themselves in work tasks when they involve the sorts of elements listed above: danger, skill, responsibility, status, than when they do not. There are limits to the axiom that when men define a situation as real it is real in its consequences.

Men who are closely involved in their work skills and tasks are likely to see themselves in terms of their occupational role, for work will be an activity which they regard as emotionally important and valuable, and the occupational role will therefore become a salient element in their self-images. Blauner has said of the American printer,

> 'the work of printers (1) will be intrinsically involving and interesting rather than monotonous; (2) will give opportunities for the expression of both present resources and skills and the development of new potentialities; (3) will be viewed chiefly as an end in itself with rewards in the actual activity, rather than as a means to satisfy future ends; (4) and will become an important and approved element of their total identity.'[28]

As well as describing the nature of printers' work and how they feel about it, this passage illustrates the relationships between involvement in work skills and tasks and the incorporation of the work role into a man's self-image. In contrast, men who view their work as a sacrifice of time and effort − as a depriving experience to be suffered in exchange for economic rewards − are not likely to see themselves in terms of their occupational role, for they will wish to escape from all the unpleasant implications of work as soon as they can.

When a group of people share a valued experience it is likely that they will develop common values based on and reflecting this shared experience, and as a result of sharing these values they will come to regard their partners in the valued activity as people whose judgements and opinions are of particular importance. Men who are deeply involved in their work skills will use their occupational fellows as a reference group.

Similarly, men who are involved in their work skills and tasks are not likely to make any sharp distinction between the two worlds of work and non-work;

---

27   Goldthorpe *et al.*, *The Affluent Worker*.
28   Blauner, *Alienation and Freedom*, p. 51.

they are likely to talk about their work outside working time and they may have work-connected hobbies or do work-connected reading, and, most important, they tend to make friends from among those who do the same work. Parker is one of many writers who have related work-based friendships to involvement in work. He says: 'Attitude to the job has an important bearing on friendship patterns . . . If work experiences are not valued, friendships are less likely to arise there.'[29] Goldthorpe *et al.* also suggest that the way men see their work is causally related to their willingness to allow work relationships and interests to carry over into their non-work lives. They say that the definite demarcation of work and non-work which was enforced by so many of their respondents, and which is so strikingly different from the attitudes of members of occupational communities, is the result of the nature of the work that these people do, and of their 'instrumental' orientation towards it.[30]

It seems most likely then that strong positive involvement in work is causally related to all three components of occupational communities. Men who take a pride in their work skills and who derive intrinsic satisfaction from practising them, are likely not only to base their self-images on their occupational role, but also to share a value system with others who share this valued activity, to choose their friends from among them and to carry work activities and interests into their non-work lives. Lipset says on this point: 'Men who are proud of their work, who view it as interesting and important, will not be "bored" with taking their jobs into their leisure time activities. A good job is a tie that binds.'[31]

The concept of marginality has had a long and varied history in sociological theory. Originally marginality was used to describe the position of a man who, though he had strong links with two ethnic groups, was not a full member of either, but was on the margin of both. Increasingly, however, the concept has been applied to the field of stratification, and research has been centred on the various sources of marginality and the various types of reaction to it. The essential feature of marginality — whether it is based on the ethnic or stratification dimension — is that people desire to belong to some group but are denied admission to it.

In the context of this discussion an occupation can be described as marginal when members identify, and wish to associate, with members of a higher-status

29   S.R. Parker, 'Type of Work, Friendship Patterns, and Leisure', *Human Relations*, vol. 17, 1964, pp. 215–19.

30   Goldthorpe *et al.*, *The Affluent Worker*, p. 53.

31   Lipset *et al.*, *Union Democracy*, p. 124.

group and when these associational ambitions are unsuccessful.[32] The American printers are a good example of such a group — their occupation is a high-status one and they therefore expect to be able to associate with members of middle-class status groups, and to avoid association with 'lower' groups. Yet for at least some of them these associational aspirations are thwarted.

Although the status level of an occupation is important as a possible factor generating involvement, it is doubtful whether it is directly related to the development of occupational communities. People who belong to an occupation which is generally accorded high status are not, because of this alone, likely to restrict their association to other members of their occupation (although they will probably base their self-image on their occupational role.) Status is only directly important as a determinant of occupational communities when there is a discrepancy between the status accorded an occupation by those involved in it and the status assessments of outsiders.

Lenski's concept of 'status crystallisation' describes one situation which might lead to marginality in our sense.[33] 'Status crystallisation' is the relationship between a man's positions on the various dimensions of status. If he has a higher position on one dimension than he has on another, then this might lead him to have associational aspirations — based on this one high position — which cannot be realised because of his lower position on the other dimension. One possible consequence of this is that such a man might find any contact outside his own group distressing and unpredictable, for there would be little mutuality within relationships. This might lead him to restrict his association to members of his own group. Lipset suggests that this is what happens with marginal occupations. Members find that they are unable to associate with people from the higher-status group and therefore prefer to associate with members of their own occupation. Such association is less distressing than association with outsiders, since members of their own occupation are prepared to confirm and support their status claims.

Marginality does not directly determine work-based self-image, yet the two phenomena are interconnected. Occupation can only be a source of marginality if members of an occupation see themselves in terms of their occupational role and feel that, for example, as printers or policemen they can claim

32 There are at least two types of marginality which are sometimes confused. First it is possible that a man's position on the various dimensions of status might not converge. This is the situation descirbed by Lenski. Secondly, it is possible that a man's status and class positions might not converge. This is also a type of marginality.

33 G.E. Lenski, 'Status Crystallization: A Non-Vertical Dimension of Social Status', *American Sociological Review*, vol. 19, 1954, pp. 405–13.

acceptance by members of higher-status groups. The relationship between marginality and self-image is a rather more complex and reciprocal one than is normally found between the determinants and components of occupational communities. It is likely that members of marginal occupations will see themselves in terms of their occupational roles, for this role probably offers the highest status and most flattering self-image available, even though some outsiders deny the legitimacy of these status claims. Men are more likely to see themselves in terms of their occupational role when that role offers a flattering self-image because of the status of the occupation; and the very essence of marginality as used here is that members of an occupation desire to associate with members of a higher-status group and are unsuccessful because they overestimate the status position of their own occupation.

Similarly, members of marginal occupations regard their occupational colleagues as the only people whose opinions and judgements matter, because only they share their view of the nature of the occupation and the 'real' statusworthiness of its members. Members of a marginal occupation share a value system which includes a definition of the importance of the job and the sort of people who do it. This is one of the *features* of marginal occupations, it is not a *consequence* of their marginality.

Marginality is, however, more clearly related to preferential association. Lipset has suggested that when members of an occupation find that their associational aspirations are frustrated, it is likely that, rather than associate with people outside the group who are seen as members of lower-status groups, they will associate with other members of their own occupation. Lipset says that 'printers view their own status as higher than that of manual workers and consequently, when unable to associate with middle-class people, prefer to associate with printers'.[34] However, there seems to be no evidence that marginality is causally related to the convergence of men's work and nonwork activities and interests; indeed it is only directly causally related to preferential association. It must be remembered, however, that the components of occupational communities are closely interrelated; anything — whether marginality or some other determinant — which affects men's friendships and associational patterns, is also very likely to affect their self-image and their reference group affiliations.

34   Lipset *et al.*, *Union Democracy*, pp. 112–13.

The extent to which occupational roles affect the non-work lives of their incumbents varies greatly.[35] Some roles 'encapsulate' their incumbents so completely that their whole lives are influenced by their incumbency of this one role. Other roles have very little effect on incumbents' lives outside their performance of specific tasks. Of course, within an occupational role the incumbent's behaviour will be largely governed by the expectations and demands of others. Gross et al., in their study of the role of the school superintendent, show this process in operation.[36] This book will attempt to classify various types of 'inclusive' factors because of which a man's non-work life can be severely affected by his work role; all have been mentioned in studies of occupational communities.

In this study interest in the various ways in which men can be affected by their work is restricted to those features of a man's occupational role which are likely to affect his non-work activities and interests and which, in particular, either restrict his opportunities to establish relationships with people outside his occupation or lead him to associate with, and make friends of, other members of his occupation. There are three types of inclusivity.

Etzioni has noted that organisations can vary in their range of *pervasiveness*, and by this he means 'the number of activities in or outside the organisation for which the organisation sets norms'.[37] Some occupations involve membership of organisations which set values and norms that are relevant to many sorts of activities. Other occupations require nothing of the incumbent beyond the execution of certain routine tasks during a set period of time. The army, for example, is an organisation that sets norms and rules which apply to many aspects of participants' lives, both in work and outside it. Janowitz writes that: 'The military profession is more than an occupation: it is a complete style of life. The officer is a member of a community whose claims over his

---

35   This section on inclusivity owes much to Etzioni. Etzioni has written that: 'Organisations differ in the degree to which they "embrace" their lower participants.' (A. Etzioni, *A Comparative Analysis of Complex Organisations* (New York, Free Press, 1961), p. 160.) He is primarily interested in types of organisational embrace, and he distinguishes these in terms of the sort of effect they have on participants' lives. He calls the two types 'pervasiveness' and 'scope'. Of the latter he says: 'Organisations differ in their scope, that is the number of activities in which their participants are jointly involved.' (Etzioni, *A Comparative Analysis*, p. 160.) In this book interest is restricted to distinguishing the mechanisms involved when men's lives are embraced by some organisation of which they are members or by certain features of their actual work situation.

36   N. Gross, W. Mason and A.W. McEachern, *Explorations in Role Analysis: Studies of the School Superintendency Role* (Wiley, New York, 1958).

37   Etzioni, *A Comparative Analysis*, p. 163.

daily existence extend well beyond his official duties.'[38] The professions are, of course, the occupational organisations with the greatest degree of pervasiveness. Recruits to such occupations experience a socialisation process during which they internalise their professional value system and thereafter they are relatively amenable to the manipulation of normative, symbolic rewards. The professional's behaviour and attitudes in many situations will be influenced by his internalisation of the professional value system.

When men are subject to a high degree of organisational pervasiveness — i.e. when they subscribe to a value system which is established by their occupational or professional organisation and which is relevant to many types of behaviour both within work and outside it — it is likely that many aspects of their non-work lives will be affected, and in particular it is likely that they will manifest a strong convergence of work and non-work activities, interests and relationships.

Etzioni has suggested that organisations may 'embrace' their participants not only through normative means but also by direct control over their action. We call this type of inclusivity *organisational embrace*.[39] Organisations which embrace their participants will attempt to 'serve as the collectivity in which many or most of an individual's activity will take place'.[40] Such organisations attempt to control many, or all, aspects of their participants' lives; they control participants' sleeping, eating and recreation, and they manage this by supplying the facilities for these activities and by ensuring that only these facilities are used. Goffman has pointed out that the organisations which exert the strongest control of this type are asylums and gaols,[41] but other organisations also subject their participants to some degree of organisational embrace. Early industrial organisations, for example, controlled many aspects of their participants' lives; but within modern western societies organisational embrace, when it occurs among industrial organisations, meets with varying reactions from the workers concerned. In some cases it merely arouses hostility and resentment.[42] Even when the organisations supply the facilities for non-work activities, few organisations in modern societies are capable of ensuring that only these facilities are used, and in most cases the workers no longer need use the facilities provided if they do not so wish, since there are others available elsewhere. Workers who manifest an 'instrumental' orientation

38   M. Janowitz, *The Professional Soldier* (Glencoe, Illinois, Free Press, 1960), p. 175.

39   Etzioni calls it scope, see Etzioni, *A Comparative Analysis*, p. 160.

40   Etzioni, *A Comparative Analysis*, p. 160.

41   E. Goffman, *Asylums* (New York, Doubleday, 1961).

42   Etzioni, *A Comparative Analysis*, pp. 164—8.

towards their work and who want to escape from it completely when they leave work, are likely to react with hostility if their employing organisation attempts to subject them to any type of organisational embrace. Members of some organisations are, however, still subject to this type of inclusivity; for example, soldiers or policemen. When it occurs it is likely to strongly influence men's non-work lives and to restrict their opportunities to establish relationships with outsiders.

There is, finally, one other type of inclusivity in which we are interested. Men's non-work lives can be affected, in the ways mentioned above, by certain features of the job itself. Such features may be called *restrictive factors*. Restrictive factors differ from organisational embrace in that, while the latter is the result of the deliberate policy of the power hierarchy within an organisation, the former are the result of the way that men's work is organised and of certain exigencies of work itself. Through their work, jazz musicians, printers, policemen and railwaymen are all subject to restrictive factors. The times when they work, and in some cases the amount of travelling they must do, make association with people outside the occupation very difficult and generally limit their non-work activities. Jazz musicians, for example, spend a lot of time travelling long distances to fulfill short-term engagements, and this makes it difficult for them to have any non-jazz musician friends; also, like printers and policemen, they work at times when other people are at rest, and this means that normal social intercourse with people other than their work companions might be very difficult.

Blakelock has shown that the times when men work may have subtle, far-reaching effects on their non-work lives. Activitites, he suggests, may be seen in terms of their flexibility, i.e. the extent to which they can be carried out at a certain time but not at another, and time varies with 'regard to its liquidity', i.e. the number of activities that may be carried out in it. Evenings or weekends are times of high liquidity. Men whose work must be carried out at times when a variety of other activities normally take place (i.e. during most people's non-work hours) are likely to find that they are, as Blakelock puts it, 'out of phase with the rest of their social world'.[43]

Members of many occupational communities work in situations which are in some way restrictive. This does not mean, however, that members of these communities only associate with each other because they are unable to make friends with other people. As Mott points out, they could also react to this

43   E. Blakelock, 'New Look at Old Leisure', *Administrative Science Quarterly*, vol. 4, 1960, pp. 446–67.

restrictive situation by having few friends, or no friends at all.[44] Nor does it mean that the men who are subject to restrictive factors and who are friends with their work colleagues will necessarily view their relationships with their work colleagues as the result of these restrictive factors. Marcus has said that the meaning of interaction to those concerned might be affected by the context within which it occurs. This is particularly evident, for example, when men are engaged in dangerous activities, but Marcus suggests that it can also occur whenever the environment is in some way unusual. 'Environment becomes a crucial determinant of group life when members define it as other than normal.'[45] When this occurs, the relationships between members of the group are likely to assume a special importance to the men concerned. Night work or working at weekends or during holiday periods, when most people are not working, are abnormal working times and might lead the people concerned to see their relationships with their fellow workers as having a special significance and as therefore forming the basis for out-of-work relationships.

Of the three types of inclusivity only the first — organisational pervasiveness — is directly related to men basing their self-image on their occupational role. Organisational pervasiveness means that members of an organisation internalise a value system and incorporate the relevant role into their self-image. Writers on the professions — the occupations which are most characterised by a high degree of organisational pervasiveness — have stressed that identification with the professional role is one of the defining characteristics of professionals.[46]

Similarly, only pervasiveness is directly related to the use of the occupation as a reference group. If members of an occupation are subject to a normative system which they internalise, then this will mean that their occupational group is a reference group for them, for they share a set of values. Mack has pointed out that when an occupational role is 'determinate', i.e. when it involves acceptance of a normative system, other incumbents of the role will become a reference group: 'Persons in determinate roles will tend to have one reference group . . . They will consider their peers the only persons competent to judge them.'[47] This is supported by the study of the jazz musicians' occupational community.

44   P.E. Mott, F.C. Mann, Q. McLoughlin and P.P. Warwick, *Shift Work: The Social, Psychological and Physical Consequences* (University of Michigan Press, 1956), p. 21.

45   P. Marcus, 'Expressive and Instrumental Groups: Towards a Theory of Group Structure', *American Sociological Review,* vol. 66, 1960, pp. 54—9.

46   Goode, 'Community within a Community'; and G. Strauss, 'Professionalism and Occupational Associations', *Industrial Relations,* vol. 2, 1962, pp. 7—31.

47   R.W. Mack, 'Occupational Determinateness', *Social Forces,* vol. 35, 1956, pp. 20—35.

Organisational embrace and restrictive factors are only related to the first two components of occupational communities through their effect on people's friendship and associational patterns. These two types of inclusivity certainly restrict men's opportunities to get to know people outside their occupation or organisation and also affect the sorts of activities that are possible in their non-work time, but it is possible that they also, under certain conditions, result in men making friends from among their occupational colleagues.

When a group of men are all subject to organisational pervasiveness as professionals are, it is highly likely that they will, because of the values and attitudes which they have in common, make friends of, and associate with each other. It is also likely that they will not attempt to separate their work and non-work lives, but will carry work activities and interests, as well as relationships, into their non-work lives.

Relationships Among the Determinants: Relative Causal Importance

These determinants are derived from a close survey of the literature on occupational communities; the factors are those which are mentioned by the authors of these studies as the determinants of occupational communities. This book aims to draw together the many scattered and disparate statements and to form a systematic model of the factors which have been regarded as the determinants of occupational communities. I am consequently prepared to hypothesise about the nature of the relationships among the determinants and the relative causal importance of each.

As far as it is possible to tell, there are no known cases of occupational communities caused by just one of these determinants; in every case at least two are present. Furthermore in every known case one of these determinants is involvement, and in so far as the studies supply the relevant data it seems that *there are no known cases of occupational communities where members are not strongly and positively involved in their work skills and tasks* (although some of the studies contain more information on this than others).

However, it seems that involvement *alone* is not a sufficient causal factor, and that at least one other determinant must also be present. Two studies of manual workers have shown that workers who are involved in their work skills, but who are not, as far as one can tell, subject to any of the other determinants, do not have an occupational community. Ingham has shown that among his sample of manual workers who were involved in their work, preferential association was still uncommon;[48] and Goldthorpe *et al.* have suggested that a similar pattern is demonstrated by the workers in their sample who were

48   G.K. Ingham, *Size of Industrial Organisation and Worker Behaviour* (Cambridge University Press, 1970).

involved in their work but were not apparently subject to any of the other determinants.[49]

There is also evidence that if men are not involved in their work, then, regardless of what other determinants are present, there is not an occupational community. It is clear from Terence Morris' study of Pentonville prison wardens that as a group they are subject to at least two types of inclusivity and there are also grounds for believing that they are a marginal group, yet they are not involved in their work and they do not have an occupational community. In fact the wardens said that the *lack* of neighbourliness among the officers was one of the unpleasant features of the job, and half the sample said that they relied solely on friends from outside their work as a source of primary contacts.[50]

Similarly, Sykes has pointed out in a recent article that navvies are subject to severe restrictive factors in their work, but are not in any way involved in their work skills and tasks, and show a marked degree of individualism and a remarkable lack of preferential association. Sykes also notes that members of this occupation share certain occupational values and hold occupational self-images, at least while they are living together in the work camps.[51]

Involvement in work skills and tasks is, it is suggested, a *necessary* but not a *sufficient* causal factor in the determination of occupational communities. This is a hypothesis which is to some extent supported by Gerstl, for he says that, holding other factors constant: 'Highly committed groups would be more likely to develop occupational communities than would those with low commitment.'[52] It is suggested that marginality and the various types of inclusivity are only causally important when allied with involvement.

Types of Occupational Community

Finally, occupational communities may usefully be separated into two types: the local and the cosmopolitan. Merton first made this distinction and it has since been used by Gouldner and Reissman among others. Merton, in his analysis of patterns of influence in the town of 'Rovere', identified two types of influential which differ from each other in the breadth of their outlook or orientation.

'The chief criterion for distinguishing the two (types of influential) is their orientation towards Rovere. The localite largely confines his

49   Goldthorpe *et al.*, *The Affluent Worker.*

50   Morris and Morris, *Pentonville,* pp. 73–101.

51   Sykes, 'Navvies'.

52   Gerstl, 'Determinants of Occupational Community', p. 46.

interest to this community. Rovere is essentially his world . . . he is preoccupied with local problems, to the virtual exclusion of the national and international scene . . . Contrariwise with the cosmopolitan type. He has some interest in Rovere . . . But he is also orientated significantly to the world outside Rovere, and regards himself as an integral part of that world.'[53]

Reissman and Gouldner have applied this distinction to members of organisations. These two writers have suggested that members of organisations may be classified into two types on the basis of, among other criteria, whether they use a reference group composed only of the people in their organisation or composed of all members of their occupation.[54]

This classification of the local and the cosmopolitan, which implies that the local is someone who is orientated towards and interested in the immediate, local world of either his town or his work place, and that the cosmopolitan is orientated towards and interested in the wider world of either the 'national or internation scene' or his occupation as a whole, can be applied to occupational communities. Although the studies of occupational communities contain few data that are directly relevant to this classification, they do suggest that some occupational communities contain the occupation as a whole, while others are composed only of those members of an occupation who share a specific work situation. The detailed characteristics of the two types of occupational community will now be set out. It must be stressed that there is no suggestion that all occupational communities are of one type or the other; there are sure to be intermediate types.

Cosmopolitan occupational communities are based on the occupation as a whole, and not just on some section of it. Such communities are composed, at least potentially, of *all* members of the occupation. Members of cosmopolitan occupational communities, like Merton's cosmopolitan influential type, are not primarily interested in their particular work situation (or geographical area in the case of the influential) but are orientated rather towards the world outside — the world of their occupation or profession as a whole.

Occupational communities involve the use of a primary reference group based on the occupation. In the case of cosmopolitan occupational

---

53   R.K. Merton, *Social Theory and Social Structures* (New York, Free Press, 1957), p. 393.

54   L. Reissman, 'A Study in Role Conceptions in Bureaucracy', *Social Forces,* vol. 27, 1949, pp. 306–31; and A.W. Gouldner, 'Cosmopolitans and Locals: Towards an Analysis of Latent Social Roles', *Administrative Science Quarterly,* vol. 2, 1957, pp. 281–306.

communities the reference group is the occupation as a whole. Professionals, for example, feel that because of the values they share with all other members of their occupation only their professional peers are able to fully understand their problems, etc., and they are likely to resent any attempt on the part of an outsider to influence the execution of their valued professional skills. Professionals and members of other cosmopolitan occupational communities share a value system with all members of their occupation and not just with those with whom they work.

Members of cosmopolitan occupational communities will tend to associate with, and make friends of, members of their occupation with whom they do not work. Their preferential association will not be limited to their colleagues. Of course, members of cosmopolitan occupational communities will have some colleague friends who also work with them but most of their colleague friends will be either people who once worked with them but who do so no longer, or people with whom they have never worked but whom they met elsewhere – often at college.[55] Members of cosmopolitan communities will be friends with occupational colleagues who do not work with them. This is their most important distinguishing feature.

Cosmopolitan occupational communities will probably differ from local ones in other ways. For one thing it is unlikely that a community which is based upon the occupation as a whole, and which involves friendships with colleagues rather than with work-mates, will be restricted to any particular geographical area in the way that some communities are.

Local occupational communities are composed not of all members of the occupation, but of those members who share a specific work situation. People who share a work situation are employed and controlled by the same authority, and if they do not actually work along-side each other, they meet frequently during working hours; they are, in fact, work-mates. Local occupational communities differ from cosmopolitan ones in certain ways, the most important of which are the type of preferential association manifested by the members and the types of occupational reference group they use.

Members of local occupational communities have friends who do the same work, but these people are their work-mates; their colleagues and friends are people who share their work situation. Members of such communities are rarely friendly with non-work-mate colleagues. Similarly, members of such communities have an occupational reference group composed not of all members of the occupation but of those colleagues who share their work situation.

55   It seems that Parker is the only writer who has thought of distinguishing friends from work from friends who are in the same occupation but who do not share a work place. (Parker, 'Type of Work'.)

If an occupational community is composed of members of an occupation who share a specific work situation, then it is likely that it will have a definite geographical location and that members — who work together — may also live together. Also, if an occupational community is composed of people who share a work situation, then members are likely to know many, if not all, the other members, and it is likely that their work-mate friends will be friendly with each other. On the other hand, if an occupational community is composed of all the members of an occupation, then it is less likely that members will know many of the other members and unlikely that their colleague friends will know each other.

Finally, it is suggested that the structure of an occupational community, i.e. whether it is local or cosmopolitan, is causally related to the particular pattern of determinants which is operative in each case. It has already been suggested that involvement in work skills and tasks is a necessary but not a sufficient determinant of occupational communities and that one other determinant, at least, must also be present. It is this 'second' determinant which is causally related to the structure of the community.

In the case of a local occupational community, which is composed of members of an occupation who share a specific work situation, the 'second' determinant will be certain features of this shared work situation — either restrictive factors or some type of organisational embrace — which so limit the associational opportunities of the men concerned that they find it difficult if not impossible to establish or maintain relationships with people who are not their work-mates.

In the case of a cosmopolitan occupational community, which is composed, at least potentially, of all members of an occupation, the 'second' determinant will be some feature of the occupation as a whole — either organisational pervasiveness stemming from some organisation of which all members of the occupation are members, or marginality — which limits the associational choices of the members of the occupation to all other members of the occupation, in as much as they will regard their occupational peers as the only people who are suitable as friends and as the people with whom they have most in common.

It is likely that there is a class link here: organisational pervasiveness implies a long training period leading, in most cases, to relatively well paid jobs. It is probable that middle-class occupational communities will have organisational pervasiveness as a determinant.

3
A review of some accounts
of occupational communities

The aims of this chapter are twofold: first, to acquaint readers with some of
the wealth of information that exists on this sort of work/leisure relationship,
and second, to begin to show how the model presented in the previous
chapter might be of some use in organising this material. The data presented
are not original, but were culled from various sources.

The Shipbuilders
The study from which the data below were drawn was not originally conceived
or designed in order to investigate Tyneside shipbuilders as an occupational
community, though this formed an interesting feature of the analysis. The
study set out to examine the nature of the shipbuilders' social imagery and
how this was related to the various aspects of their work situation. This section
is based on two articles by R. Brown and P. Brennen.[1] The study is of the
shipbuilding community of Wallsend, where, of those employed in 1964, 30
per cent were in shipbuilding and repair and 19 per cent marine engineering.
The headquarters of Swan Hunter Shipbuilding is based at Wallsend and
employs about 3,000 men.

The authors are quite certain that the Tyneside shipbuilders do constitute
an occupational community — what they refer to as a traditional working-
class community. Certain features of the shipbuilders' non-work activities and
relationships are mentioned to support this suggestion.

One feature is that the shipbuilders maintain 'close knit networks of kin,
friends, neighbours, and workmates'.[2] This means that people meet each other
in a number of different situations, one of which is the work situation. The
authors report that 'Amongst the sample of ship-building workers 55 per cent

1   Richard Brown and Peter Brennen, 'Social Relations and Social Perspectives
    Amongst Shipbuilding Workers', Part I, *Sociology,* vol. 4, 1970, pp. 71–84.

    Richard Brown and Peter Brennen, 'Social Relations and Social Perspectives
    Amongst Shipbuilding Workers', Part II, *Sociology,* vol. 4, 1970, pp. 197–211.

2   Brown and Brennen, 'Social Relations', Part I, p. 73.

had at least one friend working in the same firm.' They continue, 'The initial contact has most frequently been made through living in the same neighbourhood, working for the same firm, kinship or membership of the same club.'[3] Furthermore, these ties were important in keeping people in the work or area, and attracting them to the work in the first place. It is also stated that 'a third of all friends mentioned by shipbuilding workers were employed by the same firm as themselves, and work place was the second most important initial source of contact with friends (after locality).'[4] The shipbuilders display a close relationship between their work and non-work associates and friends.

It is also suggested that shipbuilders' leisure activities are closely based on their work, in as much as they take place in the company of friends from work. Also, of course, free time at work is likely to be spent in games or gossip.

With regard to the attitudes and orientations of the shipbuilders, a number of interesting similarities were found. Shipbuilders' attitudes towards their work are complex and differentiated (as must be true of members of so many occupations). While generally unfavourable to top management (48 per cent) they tended to be more favourably inclined towards their immediate boss. More interesting from the point of view of this book are their feelings about their work. Here it seems that the *work itself* was seen as a source of satisfaction[5] and *extrinsic* features were seen as responsible for dissatisfaction. Although changes have taken place in shipbuilding, the authors stress that basically it still has a craft technology – i.e. lack of standardisation and a low level of mechanisation and rationalisation. Most shipbuilders are skilled workers. 'Even though a great deal of equipment is supplied by outside subcontractors, the building of a ship depends essentially on the manipulation of tools and materials by men who have acquired craft skills over a number of years.'[6] This means of course that entry to the job is through apprenticeships. The authors also suggest that building ships is intrinsically an involvement-arousing activity. It is an emotional business. Although the work may be hard, uncomfortable, noisy and even dangerous, the shipbuilders' tasks 'are not as

---

3   Brown and Brennen, 'Social Relations', Part I, p. 74.

4   Brown and Brennen, 'Social Relations', Part I, p. 75.

5   Apparently this was particularly true of the apprentices who emphasised the intrinsic aspects of their work and the enjoyment they would derive from exercising the skills they were learning. This is particularly important in that it is likely to be a realistic orientation since so many of the apprentices knew, or were related to, people already in the work.

6   Brown and Brennen, 'Social Relations', Part II, p. 197.

meaningless and unsatisfying, nor as barren of any possibility of self-expression or self-development, as they are in many industrial situations'.[7] Building a ship arouses involvement.

It is argued that this involvement in work encourages the development of friendships between the shipbuilders. Shared participation in a significant activity encourages the development of close relationships. When work-mates might also be neighbours the possibility is even further increased. As they put it:

> 'The shared experience of working on a product whose manufacture is capable of involving workers beyond the limits of the wage contract, the danger and tough physical conditions associated with shipyard work and the ties of friendship which exist within the yard and extend beyond it into the wider community would seem to argue the existence of a close, solidaristic community.'[8]

The shipbuilders not only share an involvement-arousing work experience. They also share a work-based culture. As we have seen, the majority (two-thirds) of shipbuilders are skilled men who have undergone a five-year apprenticeship. During this time they have absorbed a lot more than craft skills. They have also picked up ways of defining work and the craft group. The authors refer to Eldridge, who has suggested that common norms and values are internalised through patterns of recruitment and training.[9] This craft culture has many aspects. Most important, it includes concepts of class (not the expected 'traditional' working-class models), definitions and expectations of the work and trade unions, and so on. (It is very likely that further investigation would reveal many more aspects of this work-based culture.)

The authors also point out that the occupational community of Wallsend shipbuilders is not only characterised by solidaristic relationships. Indeed one of the striking aspects of these workers is the ambivalence between inter-skill disputes and bickering and occupational homogeneity. They suggest that this is due to features of their work situation. The factors which arouse involvement lead to the development of solidaristic, friendship relationships, but at the same time they are encouraged by status and pay differentials to emphasise differences between occupations and skill levels. As a result of the tension between these aspects of their work situation shipbuilders' social imagery has

7   Brown and Brennen, 'Social Relations', Part II, p. 199.

8   Brown and Brennen, 'Social Relations', Part II, p. 204.

9   Brown and Brennen, 'Social Relations', Part II, p. 200. The reference is to J.E.T. Eldridge, 'The Demarcation Dispute in the Shipbuilding Industry', *Industrial Disputes* (London, Routledge and Kegan Paul, 1968).

a greater complexity than that usually ascribed to traditional working-class groups.

To conclude this short discussion of the community of the Wallsend ship-builders, certain points do emerge. First, the shipbuilders interact with work-mates outside working hours. There exists a close relationship between work and non-work life, activities and relationships. Secondly, the shipbuilders share a work-derived culture which includes a definition of the way in which society is stratified. Thirdly, they are closely involved in their work skills and activities: work is meaningful and intrinsically satisfying.

The Police

An occupational community is, in very general terms, one in which the worlds of work and non-work are closely interdependent, each world per-meating and affecting the other. From the available evidence policemen display this sort of work/non-work convergence in an extreme form. Indeed this is one of the main points made in two recent discussions of the police in this country — Banton's *The Policeman in the Community* [10] and Maureen Cain's 'On the Beat'.[11]

What form does this inter-meshing of work and non-work take? There are a number of areas involved. In the first place the occupational role of police-men is one that has implications for the off-duty lives of its incumbents. In-deed it could be claimed — and probably would be by some policemen, among others — that the separation of on- and off-duty hours is meaningless in the police force. Officers are not likely to disregard some serious misdemeanour just because they are off-duty. (Though it is likely that they will be more prepared to overlook minor offences: their discretionary threshold will probably be higher.)

The role of policemen is a 'determinate' one in that, like priests, doctors, etc., its incumbents are expected to behave in certain ways even when they are not 'at work' in the literal sense. These expectations are held by other in-cumbents of the role, by the role player himself and by his public. They are not, of course, necessarily very specific or detailed, nor are they necessarily totally consistent, nor will they always be held by all the various groups with equal firmness. Nevertheless, they are likely to exist. Banton quotes a policeman as saying:

10   Banton, *The Policeman in the Community*.
11   Maureen Cain, 'On the Beat: Interactions and Relations in Rural and Urban Police Forces', in Stan Cohen (ed.), *Images of Deviance* (Harmondsworth, Penguin, 1971), pp. 62–97.

'You can never get away from being a police officer. If you become a member, say, of a bowling club, invariably you'll get the remark "Here, watch what you're saying. The police are here." That always crops up. You can never walk in as John Citizen.'[12]

One reaction to this sort of situation is described by Goffman in his article on 'Role Distance',[13] in which he describes the ways people attempt to distance themselves from some of the identity-giving elements of role behaviour, by saying, in effect: 'although I'm doing what surgeons (or policemen) do, don't make the mistake of thinking that I'm exactly like all other surgeons or that I take this too seriously. Or that this is all there is to me. I'm not just a surgeon I'm also a man like other men, a father, a husband, etc.' This mechanism is likely to be used by policemen in their efforts to escape from what they think to be widely held public stereotypes of what policemen are like. Banton quotes a policeman as saying:

'I remember being in a boarding house up at Arbroath and it was nice and sociable until someone asked my wife what I did, and as soon as the police were mentioned you could sense the change of atmosphere. It took me until the next night to show that I was on holiday and that at least I'd forgotten for fourteen days that I was a policeman. I got on alright after that, but I had to make a conscious effort to overcome what happens to you then.'[14]

Because of the nature of police work it is likely that members of their various publics will be, at the very least, wary of them as associates and friends. This is probably particularly true of working-class people. Again Banton quotes supporting evidence. The reasons for this possible wariness and rejection are complex and will be discussed later, but certainly the nature of the policeman's work — as enforcer of the law — must have some significance. For this means not only that they are always on duty, always on the watch for legal misdemeanours, but that they are likely to enforce a legal system which differs in many respects from everyday notions of right and wrong, of what is seen to *really* constitute a crime, and what is merely a normal, everyday practice — 'what everybody does', etc. As associates and friends policemen are something of an unknown quantity. They bring at least a possible unpredictability, an uncertainty, into interactions because they represent a formal, legalistic view of the law, a view which differs from everybody else's.

12   Banton, *The Policeman in the Community,* p. 199.

13   Goffman, 'Role Distance'.

14   Banton, *The Policeman in the Community,* p. 200.

When it is argued that the policeman's occupational role is highly determinate, this involves more than non-policemen's reactions to him as associate or friend; it also means that the policeman's non-work life is in some respects dominated by his job. There are a number of aspects to this. In the first place, policemen are expected to be always on duty. If they are to take their work seriously and do it efficiently then they must be prepared to enforce the law outside of duty hours.[15] Secondly, policemen are subject to a number of rules which govern certain aspects of their non-work lives. These regulations specify certain activities that they and their families may not indulge in: as Banton says,

> 'The regulations are wide-ranging in the matters they cover. The first of them defines as an offence: "Discreditable conduct, that is to say, if he acts in a disorderly manner or any manner prejudicial to discipline or likely to bring discredit on the reputation of the force or the police service."'[16]

These regulations cover, or can be taken to cover in their effect, choice of associates, part-time working, and so on.

This control over policemen's non-work lives is not merely normative and prescriptive, it is also sometimes practical. In some areas they are housed together. This is an issue on which policemen have mixed feelings.

Obviously, these two aspects of the determinate nature of the policeman's occupational role: the reactions of others to policemen in terms of their being policemen instead of their other identities, and the control of policemen's non-work lives by a code of regulations, by always being on duty, etc., are closely interconnected.

---

15 Banton writes:
  'The policeman's powers and obligations are with him twenty-four hours a day and he is supposed to take official action at any time he sees a breach of the peace. When he meets an acquaintance on a sociable occasion it is difficult for either of them to forget that he is a policeman and that at some future time the policeman might have to take official action against the other. This leads to all sorts of problems. The policeman wonders whether, if such an occasion were to arise, the other man would embarrass him by expecting special treatment. For fear of such possibilities the policeman may be reserved and this may make the other man think he is being superior. Then again, the policeman frequently possesses confidential information about members of the public and could damage a few reputations if he were so minded. His occupation affects his leisure-time social relations in myriad ways and it is clearly important both for the performance of his official duty and for his own peace of mind that his public and private roles should be kept separate.' Banton, *The Policeman in the Community*, p. 189.

16 Banton, *The Policeman in the Community*, p. 192.

Another element in the close relationship between policemen's work and non-work lives (and this too follows from what has already been said) is that policemen tend to choose their friends from among their colleagues. This is demonstrated by Banton,[17] from whom table 3.1 is reproduced.

Table 3.1 *Friendships within the force*

	None	Few	More than three
City	16	18	66
Burgh	30	13	57
County	37	13	50

Note: Figures are expressed as percentages for the type of force.
Source: M. Banton, *The Policeman in the Community*, p. 248.

This table shows that two-thirds of the sample of city policemen had more than three policemen among their friends — a remarkably high proportion by any standard. Both Banton and Cain agree in noting the high level of preferential association among policemen, and both mention that city policemen seem to display a higher level than county officers. A number of reasons for this are suggested. Banton says:

'it should be borne in mind (a) that county officers are frequently moved from station to station, making the formation of any new friendship difficult; (b) that often several friends join the police together and remain friends, but that their ties have not been created after joining; (c) that as city officers work shifts it is easier to make up a foursome for golf or a party to go fishing from policemen working the same shift than from non-policemen.'[18]

Cain has added that the difference in the relationship patterns of city and county policemen was due to differences in the work situation of the two groups. County policemen have less need to rely on their colleagues, Cain argues, and this affects their friendships with them.

Certainly there are close links between the strong colleague bonds that exist between policemen and their friendship relationships. This colleagueship is founded, as Banton and Cain have pointed out, on the shared trust that

17   See also Cain, 'On the Beat', p. 78.
18   Banton, *The Policeman in the Community*, pp. 248–9.

exists among police officers. Policemen must be able to rely on their colleagues in at least three respects: firstly in cases of physical violence; secondly, in solidaristic secrecy against senior officers and the courts (this might sound ominous, and no doubt is in many instances, but it must be remembered that this is not so different from the behaviour of members of other occupations, notably, of course, the medical profession). Thirdly, the police need to depend on each other in the maintenance of the informal, unofficial and, in some cases, forbidden aspects of their work. Cain quotes a policeman who states that police recruits are not accepted as fully reliable members of the force — as proper colleagues — until they can be relied upon in these matters.

Colleagueship involves sharing values, attitudes, knowledge and expectations. It is frequently evident in the remarks which are typical of members of many occupations, that 'we're a race apart', or that 'other people just don't understand what it means to be a policeman'. The point being made when people speak like this — and it is common among members of occupational communities — is that they share a culture, a work-based world-view with their colleagues which enables them to take a great deal for granted in interactions or at work, and which they do not share with outsiders.

This occupational culture contains cognitive and cathectic elements. Cain discusses, for example, the way in which city policemen in her sample divided the community into two categories: people like 'us' and people who are so different they cannot be understood. These categories are further subdivided. This point is developed by Jock Young in his article 'The Role of the Police as Amplifiers of Deviancy . . .'[19]

Newcomers to the police force go through a training in this work-based culture. They just learn to see things the way other policemen see them — and this will actually involve learning to perceive situations in a new and unusual way.

A number of reasons why the policeman's community is an occupational one have been discussed already — the fact that policemen are subject to a body of disciplinary rules which govern certain aspects of their non-work behaviour, the fact that the nature of police work means that policemen and the public are likely to be wary of the possible implications of friendship or associational relationships, that they are expected to be always on duty.

To some extent the policeman's occupational community results from the difficulty that he experiences — or expects to experience — in his dealings with outsiders. Banton quotes from the Royal Commission on the Police to show that two-thirds of the sample of policemen said that they had experienced

---

19   J. Young, 'The Role of the Police as Amplifiers of Deviancy . . .', in Cohen (ed.), *Images of Deviance,* pp. 27–61.

difficulty in making friends with people outside the force. Over half said that they thought the public 'were reserved, suspicious, and constrained in conversation'.[20]

Banton supplies further evidence of the difficulties that policemen encounter. He asked his sample if they would reveal or conceal their occupation when on holiday. Many said that they would avoid revealing their occupational identity, and others said that they would hope it wasn't discovered.

A further reason for the policemen's social segregation is the times when they work. Like other shift-workers they work while others are asleep or at leisure. This probably has a constraining effect.

Banton also suggests that the fusion of policemen's work and non-work lives is to a great extent the result of policemen's involvement in their work. As he says, 'for most policemen work is a central life interest. They cannot stop when the hooter blows but must invest much of their personality in their duties.'[21]

Their orientation to work is not instrumental, but expressive: they feel they must learn to categorise and type people in new ways, they must learn new definitions of old situations as well as of new ones. They must in fact learn a new world-view. They must also learn and become involved in a new value system which, like all occupational value systems, is concerned with the sort of relationships members of the occupation *should* have with certain groups, notably their occupational colleagues (loyalty, trust, etc.), their officers, their colleagues in other areas or specialities, and their 'customers' – criminal and non-criminal; and to specify the real nature of policemen's work – how it should be done, and why it is important. There is evidence for this assertion, but it is scattered and diffuse. Banton makes it clear that policemen share certain ways of categorising people as well as views about how policemen should exercise their discretion, which is as one of them remarks, 'just something you pick up'.[22] Banton also mentions how junior policemen must be relied upon to use their common sense. The problem then is: 'How . . . can you teach a man common sense? Either he has got it or he hasn't. The usual policy is to rely upon his picking up the general principles by accompanying more senior men.'[23] What they pick up is, among other things, the 'police mind' or the 'police angle'. Banton points out that until the recruit learns all this he is held to be either unreliable or stupid: 'The most common complaint

20   Banton, *The Policeman in the Community*, p. 198.
21   Banton, *The Policeman in the Community*, p. 233.
22   Banton, *The Policeman in the Community*, p. 139.
23   Banton, *The Policeman in the Community*, p. 143.

of supervising officers in urban police departments seems to be of what they consider as the stupidity of some of their younger officers, whose lack of judgement creates problems for their colleagues and supervisors.'[24] This lack of judgement often involved applying the law too literally.

Cain is more explicit. She writes:

> 'The policemen, or uniformed beat men at least, emerge from this analysis as part of a highly integrated and largely defensive group which has built up a considerable number of shared definitions of situations and standards of behaviour, and which has mechanisms whereby it can resist change and indoctrinate new recruits.'[25]

In such a situation it would be surprising if policemen did not also tend to incorporate this occupational title and its concomitant world-view into their self-images and see themselves as policemen, and as people with certain qualities. Again there is some evidence from Banton to support this. He quotes one police officer who feels that policemen are recognisable even when off-duty: 'There's the height, there's the cut of your jib, there's just something they can recognise right away.'[26]

It is clear then that in many respects policemen's work permeates their non-work lives, and this has three inter-related aspects: relationships, values, which includes shared attitudes and definitions of situations, and identity.

The Fishermen

The third occupation which I shall briefly describe is that of Hull fishermen. This 'extreme' occupation has been the subject of a good deal of sociological investigation, and this treatment will draw on two studies which have different objectives and approaches but share a central interest in Hull trawlermen and their work. The studies are Jeremy Tunstall's *The Fishermen*[27] and Gordon Horobin's 'Community and Occupation in the Hull Fishing Industry'.[28]

What are the salient aspects of the fishermen's community that emerge from these works? The first is a strikingly close intermingling of the worlds of work and non-work. This is not to deny that in their leisure time they display

24   Banton, *The Policeman in the Community*, p. 139.

25   Cain, 'On the Beat', p. 95.

26   Banton, *The Policeman in the Community*, p. 198.

27   J. Tunstall, *The Fishermen: The Sociology of an Extreme Occupation* (London, MacGibbon and Kee, 1969).

28   G.W. Horobin, 'Community and Occupation in the Hull Fishing Industry', *British Journal of Sociology*, vol. 8, 1957, pp. 343–56.

what Parker[29] calls an 'opposition' work/leisure relationship; but it is to stress that when the fishermen are ashore they inhabit a world of relationships and culture that relates directly to their work activity. They will spend their time with other fishermen, for example, and live in an area — Hessle Road — where neighbours are likely to be members of the same occupation. The geographical aspect of the Hull fishermen's community has been frequently remarked upon. It is not simply the result of expediency or convenience. Horobin writes:

> 'In this area, there lives a group of people, united not only by the bonds of spatial contiguity, but by a common dependence upon one industry; an industry which, moreover, is essentially different from any other, and which by its nature affects the whole social life of its workers. This occupational bond is often reinforced by the bonds of biological and social kinship, so that the whole area appears very closely knit.'[30]

Which aspects of the job affect fishermen's social lives? Obviously the most important point is that each trip keeps them away from home for three weeks or so. Between each trip there is a turnround period which might be as short as two and a half days. As a result the fisherman's attitudes and language and beliefs and activities are likely to be deeply influenced by his work. As Tunstall puts it: 'While the ordinary shore worker can be regarded as making brief excursions to his place of work for 40 or so of the 168 hours of the week, the fisherman's life is the other way about — he makes brief excursions to the shore from his trawler, his place of work, where the majority of his time is spent.'[31]

But clearly this isn't all. Fishermen's work is also highly dangerous, uncomfortable, depriving and arduous. Nobody who has read Tunstall's account of the work of trawlermen can have any doubts that it is a job quite unlike any other. It is also the most dangerous work in Britain.[32] Eighteen-hour shifts manoeuvring trawling gear in heavy seas, soaked with freezing spray; or

---

29   Parker, 'Type of Work'.

30   Horobin, 'Community and Occupation', p. 348.

31   Tunstall, *The Fishermen*, p. 131.

32   'In every single year since 1952 the death-rate has been higher than in coal-mining. Taking the fishing deaths in two-year periods, the death-rate has varied between being nearly twice as high (1956—57) and six times as high (1954—55). On this evidence fishing may well be the occupation with the highest industrial death-rate in Britain today.' Tunstall, *The Fishermen*, p. 70.
      This was written in 1962. Since then, of course, there has been the appalling tragedy of 1968 when three Hull trawlers went down — *Saint Romanus, Dingston Peridot* and *Ross Cleveland*.

frantically gutting the heavy fish, attempting to finish the load before the next haul is dumped on the deck, while trying to avoid the heavy waves that break over the decks: this is clearly altogether different from any other sort of work.

As such it must have enormous emotional significance for those involved. This sort of work and hours, this level of discomfort and danger, this degree of deprivation, cannot be treated instrumentally. Indeed if the fishermen were to adopt an instrumental attitude they would leave the sea immediately – as Tunstall emphasises, 'the fisherman's annual earnings are extremely high, but his basic hourly rate of pay is low – probably lower than that of almost all adult male workers in Britain today'.[33]

To say that fishermen must be involved in their work is certainly not to say that they find it satisfying or enjoyable, but to suggest that it has considerable emotional significance for them. The nature of this emotional importance is difficult to establish; it probably varies over time. The involvement of a deckie learner differs from that of a veteran trawlerman (this is an issue which is usefully analysed and discussed by Tunstall). The trawlermen are committed by their work to a view of themselves and their mates, a definition of the world and their position in it, which cannot simply be sloughed off when desired. They are enmeshed in a work-based world which, for all its implications, constitutes *their* world – their only one. This explains why, despite the evident disadvantages, fishermen find it very difficult to leave the sea.[34]

The studies quoted do not supply a great deal of data on the nature of fishermen's off-duty contacts and relationships with friends and associates – and of course, they do not need to. They obviously take place with other trawlermen. Given the short turn-round periods, the geographical segregation and the shared commitment to a distinctive culture and life-style, it would be very remarkable if fishermen did not tend to spend their time together even when ashore. And of course they do. As Tunstall says: 'His (the fisherman's) favourite relaxation is drinking, mainly with other fishermen, because only they are free all day when ashore, have the same attitude to life and the same spare cash.'[35]

That fishermen do share a distinctive set of attitudes and beliefs is clear from both Tunstall's and Horobin's studies. These attitudes are reflected in their off-duty behaviour. A deep-rooted fatalism, a conviction of the

33   Tunstall, *The Fishermen*, p. 69.
34   See Tunstall, *The Fishermen*, pp. 143–8.
35   Tunstall, *The Fishermen*, p. 137.

unalterable corruption and injustice of life as it affects fishermen, seems to constitute one aspect of this. (No doubt, as Tunstall makes clear, there is considerable justification for this view, but it also serves to reinforce the conditions that give rise to it.) Attitudes towards various groups within the fishing industry, towards specialists aboard the trawler — radio operators, engineers, galley staff, towards the trawler owners, and so on; all these form distinct clusters of easily recognised and transmitted feelings. So do the fishermen's feelings about drinking and sex, and their conviction of the prevalence of back-handers.

The Jazz Musicians[36]

Jazz musicians, as an occupational community, have been most thoroughly described by Becker.[37] His interest in members of this occupation arose because they form a deviant group, in that, 'Though their activities are formally within the law, their culture and way of life are sufficiently bizarre and unconventional for them to be labelled as outsiders by more conventional members of the community.'[38] Jazz men represent in extreme form the separate, isolated quality of all occupational communities. Becker is interested in the strains resulting from the conflict between the jazz musicians' belief in artistic autonomy and commercial survival. Jazz musicians are under constant pressure to satisfy the demands of their audience. This would mean, in many cases, sacrificing their artistic integrity, for frequently audiences demand a sort of music that jazz musicians do not want to create. Jazz musicians are of course not the only people who are faced with this sort of dilemma.[39] But Becker

---

36 Unlike the other three examples, this occupational community is an American one. But it is likely that jazz musicians in this country display a similar work—leisure relationship.

37 Becker, *Outsiders.*

38 Becker, *Outsiders,* p. 79.

39 For example Hughes says:
    'it is characteristic of many occupations that the people in them, although convinced that they themselves are the best judge, not merely of their own competence but also of what is best for the people for whom they perform services, are required in some measure to yield judgement of what is wanted to these amateurs who receive the services.' Hughes, *Men and Their Work,* p. 54.
    Mason Griff has supplied an account of what happens when a member of such an occupation abdicates his professional integrity by granting the layman authority to control his performance. See M. Griff, 'The Commercial Artist. A Study in Changing and Consistent Identities', in Maurice Stein, A.J. Vidich and David Mannin White (eds.), *Identity and Anxiety. Survival of the Person in Mass Society* (New York, Free Press, 1960), pp. 219—41.

shows how they maintain an ideology which to some extent protects them from those who might threaten their autonomy and which helps them to resolve the difficulties caused by face-to-face contact with the public.

Jazz musicians not only share a value system; they also share a distinctive life-style, and form a cohesive, tightly-knit group which is separate from the rest of society.[40] They take a pride in their separateness and their distinctiveness, because, as Becker says: 'From a sense of common fate, from having to face the same problems, grows a deviant subculture; a set of perspectives and understanding about what the world is like and how to deal with it . . .'[41] This 'set of perspectives' is, as we shall see, a feature of every occupational community, but the jazz musicians' is probably more dramatic and striking than most.

The most important problem shared by jazz musicians is that mere spectators who lack the jazz musicians' experience and skill are likely to affect and control their performance of a valued activity into which they put considerable emotional and physical energy, and in which they are highly involved, by the manipulation of economic sanctions. Becker says that jazz musicians mitigate the consequent distress by means of a 'set of perspectives' which includes the assertion that the world is divided into two opposing groups – the 'cats' and the 'squares'. The jazz musician, or 'cat' possesses a precious, mysterious, artistic gift which sets him apart from the rest of the society, the 'squares', but which makes him a brother of all others who are similarly gifted.

This 'gift' not only establishes the separation of 'cats' from the 'squares', it also establishes their superiority over other members of society, and while the 'squares' might attempt to interfere in the 'cats'' musical performance, they can never overcome their essential inferiority in matters which are important. As Becker points out: 'An extreme of this view is that only musicians are sensitive and unconventional enough to give real sexual satisfaction to a woman.'[42]

The jazz musicians feel a strong sense of identity with their occupational role, and a sense of brotherhood with other members of the occupation, for only they are able to sympathise with and understand their problems and interests. Jazz musicians are loath to associate with people outside their occupational group, and this self-imposed segregation is expressed in the actual

---

40   Two writers who have also described the jazz men's occupational community say: 'While the jazz community is characterised by a number of distinctive behaviour patterns, almost without exception these tend to cluster around one central theme – the isolation of the group from society at large, an isolation which is at once psychological, social and physical.' Mack and Merriam, 'The Jazz Community', p. 211.

41   Becker, *Outsiders*, p. 38.

42   Becker, *Outsiders*, p. 86.

playing situation, where the jazz musicians frequently attempt to place a physical barrier between themselves and their audience; a barrier which not only symbolises the cultural segregation of the 'cats' from the 'squares' and acts as a protection against their interference, but also symbolises the extent to which jazz musicians, as a result of their esoteric, separatist ideology, desire to keep any outside contact to a minimum.[43]

Becker quotes a jazz musician talking about 'squares'; he displays what is apparently a widely held view of non-jazz men: 'You know man I hate people. I just can't stand to be around squares. They drag me so much I just can't stand them.'[44]

Jazz musicians, then, see themselves in terms of their occupational role and hold a distinct and unconventional value system which stresses their superior and highly prized abilities and characteristics. Members of this occupation form a distinct and separate group within society, preferring, whenever possible, to restrict all their social contacts to other members of the occupation. Why is this?

According to Becker the primary reason for the jazz musicians' occupational community is the importance they attach to their artistic gift. Becker says: 'The gift is something which cannot be acquired through education; the outsider, therefore, can never become a member of the group.'[45] Because they share this valued musical ability jazz musicians regard themselves as separate from other members of the society and want to live apart from them. Again, to quote Becker: 'The musician thus views himself and his colleagues as people with a special gift which makes them different from nonmusicians and not subject to their control, either in musical performance, or in ordinary social behaviour.'[46]

Becker also considers that the jazz men's occupational community is to some extent the result of another determinant: the conditions of work of jazz musicians are likely to make association with outsiders — even if desired — difficult, if not impossible. The hours when jazz musicians work and the considerable amount of time they spend travelling make association with non-jazz

43   Another writer who has studied jazz musicians has noted their distinctive value system and shown how it relates to their associational isolation. He writes: 'Jazz musicians exhibit a cult-like consensus on certain aesthetic matters, employ an esoteric jargon, are neither trained nor disposed to seek similarities between their way of thinking and living and other people's.' (William B. Cameron, 'Sociological Notes on the Jam Session', *Social Forces*, vol. 33, 1954, pp. 177–82.)

44   Becker, *Outsiders*, p. 99.

45   Becker, *Outsiders*, p. 86.

46   Becker, *Outsiders*, p. 86.

men unlikely. He writes: 'the conditions of work — late hours, great geographic mobility, and so on — make social participation outside of the professional group difficult. If one works while others sleep, it is difficult to have ordinary social intercourse with them.'[47]

Conclusion

It is our contention that the four occupations described above form occupational communities in the sense outlined in Chapter 2. Indeed two of them, fishermen and shipbuilders, are very much the sort of traditional working-class community described by Lockwood (although of course, as the authors of the study of the shipbuilders point out, the shibuilders' values and social imagery do not accord with those suggested by Lockwood). Nevertheless, his general description of the traditional type of community is remarkably apposite.

> 'Workers in such industries (as mining, docking and shipbuilding) usually have a high degree of job involvement and strong attachments to primary work groups that possess a considerable autonomy from technical and supervisory constraints. Pride in doing 'men's work' and a strong sense of shared occupational experiences make for feelings of fraternity and comradeship which are expressed through a distinctive occupational culture. These primary groups of workmates not only provide the elementary units of more extensive class loyalties but work associations also carry over into leisure activities, so that workers in these industries, usually participate in what are called 'occupational communities'. Workmates are normally leisure-time companions, often neighbours, and not infrequently kinsmen. The existence of such closely-knit cliques of friends, workmates, neighbours and relatives is the hall-mark of the traditional working class community.'[48]

This is an accurate picture of the occupational communities of fishermen and shipbuilders, although it should be noted that the link between occupational community and class consciousness deriving from a them/us view of the world, as suggested by Lockwood, is by no means an inevitable feature of occupational communities, and possibly not even of all traditional occupational communities. Indeed many traditional occupational communities, especially

47   Becker, *Outsiders*, p. 97. See also Cameron's article; this writer mentions the features of jazz musicians' work which result in their isolation. Cameron, 'Sociological Notes'.

48   D. Lockwood, 'Sources of Variation in Working Class Images of Society', *The Sociological Review*, vol. 14, 1966, pp. 249–62, pp. 250–1.

those classified earlier as 'quasi' communities, are more likely to result in *parochialism* than in a sense of *national* solidaristic class consciousness.[49]

An equally strong convergence of the worlds of work and non-work is also displayed in the two other occupations, in the three respects suggested in Chapter 2: relationships, values, and culture and identity. Indeed the very segregration of members of these two occupations from other members of society forms the central theme in the shared world-view and perspective.

All this, however, should not be taken to suggest the utility of the model presented earlier, for the model itself was derived from an analysis of these occupations, among others. The job of assessing the utility of the model comes later.

49   The relationship between occupational communities of varying sorts and the
      development of class or occupational consciousness or conceptions of shared
      interests is discussed more thoroughly in Graeme Salaman, 'Occupations,
      Community and Consciousness', in M.I.A. Bulmer (ed.), *Studies in Working Class
      Imagery*, London, Routledge and Kegan Paul (forthcoming).

4
The determinants of the occupational communities of architects and railwaymen

The Nature of the Study

In this chapter and the following one, the data on the nature and determinants of the occupational communities of London architects and Cambridge railwaymen will be presented. But first a word about the aims and status of the empirical investigation. In Chapter 2, a model of a particular sort of work/ leisure relationship was put forward. A simple typology for occupational communities was suggested, and hypotheses concerning their determinants advanced. These were all derived from other studies, not from the investigation which I shall go on to describe. The suggestion is not that the authors of these studies were unwittingly using such a model and such hypotheses (although, of course, they may have been doing so implicitly), but rather that on surveying a number of these studies certain ways of ordering and classifying the work seem possible. This is what I have done.[1]

In the empirical study two occupations were examined, which on *a priori* grounds seemed to involve a remarkably close relationship between work and leisure activities, etc. They would, according to the sorts of criteria *apparently* employed by others, be worthy of the title 'occupational community',[2] and consequently were chosen for detailed investigation along the lines suggested in Chapter 2. Although such an investigation could not *verify* the propositions (for lack of time and money precluded the possibility of a comparative study, involving the investigation of a third occupation which did *not* show a strong

---

1   This is exactly what Homans does in his work *Social Behaviour.* He writes: 'The strategy I follow starts with a scanning of the literature within a particular field in search of the sheer, approximate, empirical propositions, and with an effort to state them in some single set of concepts, that is, some single set of terms.' G.C. Homans, *Social Behaviour: Its Elementary Forms,* London, (Routledge and Kegan Paul, 1961), p. 9.

2   As was noted earlier, few writers who have described occupational communities have explicitly defined the phenomenon. Those investigators who do supply a definition use preferential association as the defining characteristic and initially I used this to ensure that I was dealing with the same phenomenon.

link between work and leisure), it could be, and in the view of the author was, concerned with testing these hypotheses, at least in a negative sense. After all, if it is found that members of the two occupations do have friends from work and see themselves in terms of their work title, but do not, apparently, share any work-based beliefs or values, then the suggestion that in cases of extreme work—leisure convergence these three things tend to go together will have been shown to be false. Equally, if it is found that members of the two occupations have an occupational community (on our terms), but that the suggested determinants are not operative, then those determinants will have been shown to be irrelevant. Similarly the classification, suggested in Chapter 2, of local and cosmopolitan occupational communities is irrelevant if these two oc-cupations do not display the postulated differences; for these occupations should — again on *a priori* grounds — be representative of the two types. But if it is found that members of the two occupations have friends from work, share a work-based value system and see themselves in terms of their work title, *and* that they are involved in their work and are marginal, or subject to some sort of occupational inclusiveness, then this will suggest that on the basis of this study — which should perhaps be seen as a pilot investigation — the hypotheses are worthy of further, more rigorous testing.

The sequence of events leading to the setting up of this study is not ir-relevant to the discussion at this point and is as follows: In the first place the author had personal experience of both occupations. [3] Thus he had some access to the occupations and knowledge about them, and was familiar with some of the technical and slang terms used by architects and railwaymen. This knowledge suggested that these occupations involved a very close relationship between work and leisure. Secondly, pilot investigations revealed that architects and railwaymen did indeed have 'putative' occupational communities (i.e. they revealed the sort of work—leisure relationships which would occur in an occupational community defined according to the criteria normally and previously used). These 'putative' communities were then investigated, using the model and hypotheses suggested earlier.

The first part of the research was designed to discover whether the data from two occupations were consistent with the hypotheses concerning the determinants of occupational communities. On the basis of an investigation

---

3   From 1960 to 1961 the author was a student of architecture at Brighton Art
     College. Then he was thrown out. However, since that time he has maintained
     contacts and friendships with a number of architects. From 1961 to 1962 he
     worked for British Railways (Holyhead), and although this was on the Holyhead—
     Dun Laoghaire mail boats there were many opportunities to get to know railwaymen
     and in this way the author gained an early impression of the railwaymen's
     occupational community.

of studies of occupational communities certain factors seemed important as determinants. These are, to recapitulate: involvement in work skills and tasks, marginality and inclusivity. Although no single study of an occupational community explicitly mentions all these determinants – for one contribution of this research is that it synthesises this list from existing studies – yet it is rare for an investigator who analyses an occupational community to employ as a determinant any factor which cannot be classified among the three mentioned.[4] Two sociologists have actually shown how these determinants are causally related to the components of occupational communities. Lipset has shown that preferential association among printers was the result of their marginality and involvement in their work tasks.[5] Gerstl has done similar work.[6] However, it is not merely suggested that these three factors are causally responsible for occupational communities; the following hypothesis is also advanced: involvement in work skills and tasks is a necessary, but not a sufficient determinant of an occupational community. In any particular case *involvement and at least one other determinant are present.*

Furthermore, it has been argued that the local/cosmopolitan distinction is related to differences in the determination of the occupational community. In the case of a local occupational community the second determinant will be some feature of the specific work situation, that is members will be subject either to restrictive factors which derive from their work situation, or organisational embrace from their employing organisation. In the case of a cosmopolitan occupational community the second determinant will be some feature of the occupation as a whole, that is members of the occupation will either be in a marginal situation (with respect to their location in the stratification system), or they will be subject to organisational pervasiveness stemming from some occupational organisation to which they all belong. Assuming that we are dealing with examples of these two types, then it will also be possible to test these hypotheses.

The second part of the empirical research was designed to test the validity of the components of the model presented in Chapter 2. Did members of these two 'putative' occupational communities see themselves in terms of

---

4   There is possibly one exception to this. Banton points out in *The Policeman in the Community* that the segregation of the policeman is not due simply to his being subject to a variety of rules and restrictions and, in a sense, always on duty, both of which could be seen as types of inclusivity. Their segregation is also due to the hostile and suspicious way in which outsiders tend to treat them. If this is true it is presumably only true of policemen, and is a result of the nature of their work.

5   Lipset *et al., Union Democracy.*

6   Gerstl, 'Determinants of Occupational Community', pp. 43–5.

their occupational titles? Did they use an occupational reference group and share values with their fellows? Did they have colleague friends, was there a close relationship between their work and non-work activities and interests? Further, if the two occupations were occupational communities, were they different *types* of community, according to the sort of classification set out earlier, i.e. was one a local community, the other a cosmopolitan one? The interview schedule used was designed to bring out any such differences, should they exist.

A word about the sort of sociological perspective underlying this work is appropriate. I do not suggest that men's actions are determined simply by social forces, nor that they merely act out the dictates and logic of some external system. This research is firmly grounded in the assertion that men act according to their intentions and beliefs, but that their actions are constantly subject to existing patterns of expectations and obligations (which is not to suggest that this is necessarily a societal consensus on such expectations and obligations), and are also restricted by their position within the division of labour, the class structure. As I hope this and the following chapter will show, the behaviour, attitudes and relationships of members of the two occupational samples[7] certainly do not result from 'forces' acting upon them (although they may be the result of other *men* acting upon them). Rather they result from the ways in which men define, and have learnt through time to define, situations and experiences they are influenced by, the nature of these situations and experiences, and the ways in which they have changed. These situations and experiences moreover have an existence independent of the people who will speak in the next two Chapters.

Methodology and Sampling

Before presenting the data and assessing their significance for the hypotheses advanced earlier, it is relevant and necessary to consider the status of these data and the nature of the research design, with special reference to the possibilities of generalising from these data to the occupations overall.

First the choice of occupations. As already noted, there were certain personal reasons why the choice of these two occupations was convenient and sensible, but these alone were not sufficient to warrant this selection; our choice must be more fully justified and explained. Architects and railwaymen were chosen because, in view of the existing studies of occupational communities

---

7   Two occupational samples were selected for investigation: London architects who were members of the North West London branch of the R.I.B.A., and Cambridge railwaymen. There were, respectively, 51 and 52 respondents. The railwaymen included drivers, signalmen and guards.

and the determinants which they (implicitly or explicitly) contained, as described in Chapter 2, these two occupations seemed most likely to involve their members in occupational communities. Clearly, since the object of the study was to gather information on this phenomenon, it was highly desirable to ensure (as far as possible) that the occupations studied would involve the sorts of work/leisure relationship that were generally considered — by other writers who had studied occupational communities — to constitute what was known as an occupational community. The contribution of this study was not to *discover* two new occupational communities, but to consider their nature, and the character of the causal mechanisms that produced this sort of work/leisure link. To do this it was first necessary to find two occupational communities, and existing information on architects and railwaymen strongly suggested that the determinants isolated earlier were present.

But there was another reason for the choice: it was felt that a subsidiary, but significant contribution of this study could be to give information on two occupations that were relatively unstudied. The choice of architects and railwaymen is thus to some extent the result of the fact that there is little information on these two occupational groups.

It was neither practical nor strategic to use all the members of both occupations as the populations from which to draw the two research samples. Accordingly both populations were geographically limited and one was also limited by type of work. These parameters need exposition and justification.

It is unlikely that the geographical limitations (London architects, Cambridge railwaymen) have particular significance for the findings. The basic aim of this study was to investigate the relationship between work and leisure with particular reference to the friendship relationships of members of the occupations and the possibility of these two occupational samples displaying different types of colleague relationships (i.e. local versus cosmopolitan). The questions were accordingly concerned with investigating respondents' friends — were they from the same occupation, were they work-mates or not? For these purposes it was largely irrelevant where the respondents worked and lived, since there was no interest in investigating neighbourhood communities, and the local/cosmopolitan distinction refers not to residential propinquity, but to preparedness (or capacity) to establish relationships with others in the same occupation or others who share the same work situation — but who may, or may not, live elsewhere. In other words even if a nation-wide sample of architects and railwaymen had been used it is difficult to see how respondents' relationships with their colleagues, and/or work-mates, would have differed from the relationships reported by the respondents in this more limited study. Although, of course, such a research design would have meant that the likelihood of respondents knowing *each other* (rather than just another member of the occupation who was not in the research sample) was highly remote. In short, then, because it is argued (and the data presented later will be seen to confirm) that it is features of *work* that determine the existence and nature of occupational communities, and not merely residential propinquity, it was considered safe to limit the populations to geographical areas. However, it is true that choice of occupation has implications for area of residence, and the research samples were drawn from areas where concentrations of the two occupations were expected.

The two geographically limited populations were: drivers, signalmen, firemen and guards who came under the control and administration of British Rail, Cambridge, and all architects who were nominal members of the North West London Society of Architects. All qualified architects who lived within the North West London area were automatically members of this architectural society regardless of involvement or participation in the society or its activities. The occupational breakdown of these architects was as follows: twenty-nine were salaried architects who worked either in private-practice architects' offices, or in authority architecture departments; eleven were salaried architects who worked for building or construction firms or for other types of non-architectural firms or organisations, and twelve were private-practice principals. No attempt was made to concentrate on particular types of architectural work: the occupational breakdown of the sample was quite random.

The railwaymen's population was further limited by type of work. This restriction was not for convenience, but was a deliberate effort to maximise the possibility of studying those employees of British Rail who were most likely to be members of an occupational community. The justification for this has already been stated in discussions of the choice of architects and railwaymen as the two occupational groups — that is, because the study was an attempt to study occupational communities it made sense to ensure as far as possible that the groups studied did display in general terms this sort of work/leisure relationship. As was noted in Chapter 2, involvement in work is seen as a key factor, and involvement in work relates to the status of the work and the skills and training required, among other factors. The population of railwaymen slected for study (drivers, signalmen, firemen and guards) was felt to be suitable in terms of these intentions.

The population of railwaymen, as restricted by the above parameters, was made up of 170 railwaymen. Two pilot studies were carried out, the second being necessary because of poor response to the first pilot contacts. For the main research interviews a sample of 65 railwaymen was randomly selected from the population; 51 of these were interviewed, but of the remaining 14 only 5 actually refused to take part; the rest had moved, retired or died since the list on which the population was based had been drawn up, earlier in the year.

The population of architects as restricted by membership of the North West London Society of Architects was made up of 401 male architects. One pilot study was carried out and a random sample of 80 architects was selected from the population. Fifty-two architects were prepared to take part in the study.

Involvement in Work Skills and Tasks

It is important to emphasise the distinction between *work* and *job*. 'Work' is what a man does in his job; it refers to the activities involved in holding a particular job. A 'job' refers to an actual employment situation, and therefore includes such things as conditions of work, management—worker relations, level of pay, etc. It is interesting that as we shall see, many of the respondents made this distinction themselves.[8]

Throughout the interviews, and indeed in all the various sorts of meetings the author had with respondents from both occupations, the architects and railwaymen displayed a marked interest and involvement in their work tasks and skills. They made it very clear that work was an 'activity' that had considerable emotional importance for them. They were prepared, indeed eager, to talk at length about their work and the satisfactions and frustrations it brought them.

Some indication of respondents' feelings about their work may be gathered from their answers to the question: 'What are the things you like most about your work as an architect/railwayman?' All the architects and all but one of the railwaymen mentioned intrinsic aspects of their work; for example such things as its variety, or autonomy. *They derived satisfaction from actually doing their work.* Extrinsic aspects of the work, for example the money they were paid, or their working conditions or hours of work, were not mentioned. These non-instrumental attitudes[9] towards work differ strikingly from the attitudes held by other groups of workers.[10]

8   This distinction is very similar to one made by John Goldthorpe *et al.* See Goldthorpe *et al., The Affluent Worker,* p. 10, footnote 3.

9   An instrumental orientation means seeing something purely as a means to an end, rather than as an end in itself. See Goldthorpe *et al., The Affluent Worker.*

10   For more on these differences see the next chapter.

There was some variation in the specific sorts of intrinsic satisfactions mentioned. Tables 4.1 and 4.2 present a breakdown of these.

Table 4.1 *Sources of intrinsic satisfaction mentioned by the railwaymen*

	Railwaymen ($n = 51$)
Source of intrinsic satisfaction	Percentage mentioning each source
General performance of work tasks and duties	76.47
Variety and interest of work	49.02
Autonomy of work	35.29
Importance, responsibility of work	21.57
DNA*	11.96

* 2 per cent of the railwaymen did not mention any intrinsic work satisfaction in their answers to the original question.

Many of the railwaymen said quite simply that they enjoyed their work. Some typical responses were:

> 'I just enjoy driving, I always have done. I love being out on the road.'

> 'I like the work, because its always different and there's always more to learn; it's never the same.'

> 'You either enjoy it or you'd go under. You couldn't stand it if you didn't enjoy it. This is a real job.'

> 'It's like being the captain of a ship, your're on your own and it's up to you. There's no one can help you once you're in that cab.'

> 'This job takes time to master, but then it's not like any old job, this is a life and death business. That makes a difference you know. I wouldn't swap this for anything.'

The railwaymen in the sample did different jobs – driver, signalman, second man, guard – and so one would expect them to mention different types of work satisfactions. But in fact they tended to mention the same sorts of work-based enjoyments: responsibility, autonomy, and variety. Although of course the drivers and signalmen in particular stressed the enjoyment they derived from the exercise of their work skills and techniques, all the railwaymen felt that they played an important and necessary part in carrying out and maintaining an important and worthwhile activity. It will be clear that railwaymen's work feelings and experiences are a result of the combination of their hopes, expectations, values and self-images, and their actual work tasks and work organisation. I will discuss the way recent changes in railwaymen's work circumstances have, by opening up a gap between orientation and reality, caused their attitudes to become markedly ambivalent.

The features of architectural work mentioned by the architects are presented in table 4.2.

Table 4.2 *Sources of intrinsic satisfaction mentioned by the architects*

Source of instrinsic satisfaction	Architects (*n* = 51) Percentage mentioning each source
Creativity of work, opportunity to use design skills	63.46
Importance, responsibility of work	15.38
Problem-solving aspects or intellectual challenge of work	15.38
Administrative, managerial aspects of work	11.54
Variety of work	19.23

These data can be usefully filled out with quotations from the interviews. Some architects said simply that they enjoyed their work activity. One remarked: 'I just enjoy designing buildings, it's fascinating, challenging work.' Others were more specific:

> 'I like architecture for its completeness; you're involved in and responsible for the whole business of putting up buildings.'

> 'It's finding the solutions that's the fun in this work, not just the design solutions either, but functional, practical solutions.'

> 'The marriage of art and technology, that's what makes this job so exciting.'

The architects in the sample did different sorts of jobs, but once again there was a surprising consensus on the sources of work satisfactions. With some variations, the architects derived enjoyment from using those skills and abilities which they considered to be the essential characteristics of the architect. In most cases this involved, predictably, being involved in designing buildings in some way. But some architects did suggest that their creativity was of a more problem-solving than of a designing nature.

67

Immediately after the question on work satisfactions respondents were asked, 'What are the main things that you dislike about your work as an architect/railwayman? 'Respondents' answers are set out in table 4.3. This table shows that in answering this question many respondents spoke of certain features of their *jobs* which they found unpleasant, or which restricted their opportunity to employ their work skills, or carry out their work tasks. Their remarks about their work dissatisfactions supply further evidence of their non-instrumental attitudes towards their work. These data need further discussion. Each occupation will be analysed separately.

Table 4.3 *Features of work considered as sources of work dissatisfaction*

Type of work feature	Architects (n = 52)	Railwaymen (n = 51)
	Percentage mentioning each category	
Factors which restrict opportunities to derive intrinsic rewards	71.15	5.88
Physical or social environment	11.54	23.53
Exigencies of work (e.g. shift work, late hours, etc.)	5.77	52.94
Inadequate level of pay	1.92	5.88
Other	9.62	–
Nothing	23.08	19.61

Railwaymen
The source of dissatisfaction most commonly mentioned was shift work. Over half the sample said that they did not dislike any feature of the work itself but they did dislike having to work shifts, for this interfered with their family and social lives. The railwaymen objected not only to the actual times when they worked; they also disliked being uncertain about future working times, for this made any sort of long-term planning difficult.

The twenty-four (23.53) per cent of the railwaymen who mentioned the physical or social environment of their work as a source of dissatisfaction referred either to their actual working conditions or to the deficiencies of British Rail management. The latter was a frequent topic of conversation.

A few quotations from the interviews illustrate the railwaymen's dissatisfactions with their work.

'I don't like the way things are run today; they mess us about all the time, and you never know where you are.'

'The shift work is the only bad thing about this job, it kills the social life completely, you see.'

Table 4.3 shows that few of the railwaymen mentioned money as a source of dissatisfaction. This does not mean that they were actually happy with their level of earning, for in answer to a direct question on this (which is discussed in the next chapter) 84.31 per cent of the sample said that they thought they were inadequately paid. The point is, however, that the railwaymen did not perceive the question on work dissatisfactions in terms of money, and this further reveals their non-instrumental attitude towards their work.

It is impossible to understand railwaymen's feelings about their work without being aware of their history. Railwaymen's expectations of their work and their work situation, have been built up over time, developed and transmitted. They are now largely unrealised. Discrepancy between hope, expectation and reality is particularly acute for footplatemen. Technological changes have been most significant for the footplatemen, bringing with them changes in work relationships and activities, and changes in the organisation of railway work. This latter change affects all railwaymen to some extent.

The change from steam to diesel power has had a number of consequences for drivers and firemen (now known as second men). For one thing the drivers maintained that although diesel locomotives were easier to drive they were very much more difficult to understand. Consequently the drivers felt that they were faced with an enormously complicated piece of machinery which they merely administered; unlike driving the steam engine, they had little opportunity to affect the diesel's performance. But when they spoke of steam engines they emphasised that they had to be 'worked', and they described how the driver, and his fireman, actually 'drove' the locomotive, through skilful manipulation of and control over numerous controls and processes. There were tales of how some drivers used only half as much coal as others on the same run, and other anecdotes which stressed the importance of the driver's skill and experience in driving steam engines. The transition from steam to diesel has also, of course, had drastic effects on the fireman, who now, as the 'second man', finds himself with a totally different job — some would say a non-job.

At the same time, of course, it could certainly be argued that diesel engines require more skill, not less; and this points to the need to unpack the frequently used concept 'skilled work'. Certainly diesel engines are very much more complicated technologically, and certainly drivers are now expected to know a great deal more technical information than ever before, especially since there are a number of different sorts of diesel locomotive. Further the driver of a diesel locomotive has enormous horsepower at his control. But at the same time the driver has very much less responsibility for the performance of the engine; his part in actually getting the locomotive and train from one place to another is very much less than in the days of steam. What is more, because of the complexity of the diesel engine, drivers are forbidden to attempt any repairs to an engine that has broken down; in the days of steam they would often manage to effect adequate on-the-spot repairs to get the train home.

It was often suggested that the change in sort of power had also affected the nature of the relationship between driver and fireman. In the days of steam these two were necessarily closely interdependent in driving the engine. They depended on each other. This functional colleagueship which, in a great many cases, became a close and long-lasting relationship, is no longer. Nowadays the driver and second man interact on a completely different basis, and the functional interdependence of one shovelling coal and watching for signals and the other controlling power and steam no longer exists. Also, while in the days of steam drivers and firemen worked together, on the same engine, for long periods, now engines and men are allocated on the basis of jobs, and drivers can no longer expect to get either the same engine or the same second man. The recent change in policy which allows drivers to go out alone, without firemen, represents the final stage in the destruction of the traditional relationship.

But the other change that affected all the railwaymen was the decline in their sense of security. Many claimed that when they joined the railways it was one of the most secure and high-status working-class jobs, but now they felt that redundancies had introduced a note of anxiety and had altered the nature of the relationship between the men. Thus the sense of community, the strong solidaristic bonds between railwaymen, were threatened from two directions: the changes in the technology and organisation of work meant that footplatemen were no longer functionally dependent on each other over long periods; and changes in the national organisation and administration of the railways meant that their first concern was not the well-being of the occupation as a whole but their own individual survival within it. But despite these changes the railwaymen still (as the next chapter shows) displayed a remarkable convergence of work and non-work in many areas; although in view of the changes in technology and organisation , it seems unlikely that future generations of railwaymen will display the same sort of involvement in their work and colleagues.

Other changes have taken place that affected all the railwaymen in the sample. The relative position of railway work *vis-à-vis* other working-class jobs has deteriorated, or is thought by the railwaymen to have done so. The status of the job, and hence the pride of those who do it, has, railwaymen feel, certainly declined. The pay, compared with that of other working-class jobs, has also fallen; and the conditions of work and the shift work were increasingly felt to involve unwarranted — and unrewarded — inconveniences. Some of the railwaymen felt that their goodwill was being exploited, and that while those who had known the railways in the old days might be, to some extent, prepared to put up with the inconveniences and frustrations, they would be the last generation to do so.

Railwaymen's views about their jobs were complex and ambivalent. Their work had considerable emotional importance for them and they saw it not simply as a means of making money but in terms of a work-based identity, a source of meaningful relationships, activities and responsibilities. But at the same time they were disappointed, and anxious, as a result of changes in the work and its organisation. Uncertainty had appeared in a world where, above all else, predictability, regularity and confidence in the future had been dominant. At the same time the railwaymen would find it difficult to move to another job, even if they wanted to. For while many railway jobs require a considerable degree of skill and learning, and a willingness to take responsibility and accept a rigorous and demanding discipline, these skills are, on the whole, not transferable to other jobs. They are, in a sense, trapped in a way of seeing themselves, in an occupation which has become an integral part of their lives, which has changed and is changing in ways that affect them deeply, because of their personal investment, which they are unable to shrug off. And this, of course, is their personal tragedy.

The resulting ambivalence and individual disappointment was evident throughout the interviews, and is shown in their answers to two questions; first, 'If you had a son who showed ability and who wanted to be an architect/railwayman, would you be pleased, indifferent or disappointed?' and secondly, 'If you could start your career again, would you choose the same work?' In answer to the first question, 27.45 per cent said they would be pleased, 9.80 per cent indifferent and 62.75 per cent disappointed.

A man's reactions to his son following his occupation is a good indication of his own feelings about his job; and the majority of the railwaymen would be disappointed if their sons followed their occupational choice. Many answered this question by saying: 'I'd shoot him!' But although the majority were prepared to try and stop their sons entering their occupation many of them said that they would personally repeat *their* own choice of job, if they were to return to the time when they joined. Fifty-one (50.98) percent would join the same occupation if they could start their career again, 45.10 per cent would try another line of work and 3.92 per cent did not know. The differences between the percentage of railwaymen who would like their sons to become railwaymen (27.45) per cent and those who would themselves join the railways again,

(50.98 per cent), reflects the railwaymen's feelings about the jobs, and their past experiences and satisfactions, but also shows their frustration and disappointment at the changes that have taken place. One railwayman who was personally prepared to repeat his own choice of occupation if he was to go back thirty years to the time when he originally joined, at fourteen, said: 'The railways are finished now. It was once the best job in the world but it's nothing now. That's why I wouldn't let any son of mine go into the railways. We were the last generation to know what the railways were really like.'

Architects

Among architects dissatisfaction with their jobs was the result of their being to a greater or lesser extent unable to obtain the sorts of intrinsic satisfaction they valued. Their dissatisfactions revealed the relative nature of work attitudes: like the railwaymen, the architects saw themselves as people of a particular sort with certain highly developed skills, abilities and strengths. It came as something of a blow to them to find that they were unable, in so many cases, to employ these skills in their work. This discrepancy was very deeply and personally felt when it occurred, because of the personal investment these men had in their work-based self-image. Their personal reality, like that of the railwaymen, was, or could be, threatened.

The sources of dissatisfaction, most frequently mentioned (see table 4.3) were those factors which frustrate the architects' opportunities to design freely, without restriction or interference. Table 4.4 presents a detailed breakdown of the various work features contained in the first category ('Factors which restrict opportunities to derive intrinsic rewards') of table 4.3.

The most important and obvious point to emerge from table 4.4 is that the majority of the architects were in jobs where they were, to some extent at least, either deprived of opportunities to practise their valued professional skills, or unable to use them in the way that they would like. Secondly, as noted above, these frustrations were due to the nature of architects' work expectations, acquired during training and from other members of the profession, their personal investment in them, and their inapplicability to the realities of employment. Many of the architects mentioned government and local authority building regulations as sources of annoyance and frustration: they disliked having to constantly adjust their designs to fit into what they ofte regarded as irrelevant, antiquated bureaucratic rulings. Other architects worked in large offices where they were kept busy on other people's designs, or where they had become experts on some particular design detail and were rarely able to work on complete projects. Others were free to design but claimed that they were restricted by the interference of their clients.

One architect was quite blunt about his problems. He said: 'There's only one thing wrong with this work — clients.'

Table 4.4 *Factors which restrict architects' opportunities to derive intrinsic rewards from their work*

Type of restricting factor	Architects ($n = 52$)
	Percentage mentioning each factor
Restriction from building bye-laws, local authority restriction, etc.	23.08
Client interference	23.08
Restrictions due to the way that work is organised and administered within an office: spending time on dull jobs or on administration, etc.	19.23
Other, general restrictions	15.38
D.N.A.*	28.85

* Twenty-nine (28.85) per cent of the architects did not mention any feature of their work which restricted their opportunities to derive intrinsic rewards.

Although not all architects personally experienced difficulties with clients, most architects apparently regard such frustrations as one of the major drawbacks of the profession. In a survey of British architects Abrams found that 91 per cent of the sample thought that the general level of design in this country was bad or indifferent, and two-thirds blamed the client for this.[11] It seems likely that this finding reflects the weak position of architects and architecture in this country; their uncertainty about their occupational role; their inter-occupational competitiveness; their relative under-employment, and their consequent inability to resist or control commissions. It also reflects architects' vestigial attachment to historical views of the nature of architecture: the architect as an artist, hampered and harried by his patron.

Like the railwaymen the architects mentioned various changes in the organisation of architecture and building technology, and design methods, which they felt to be undermining architects' professional role. These changes all involved either a reduction in the design function of the architect (system building, large-scale architect's offices) or intrusions into the role of the architect by other occupations (design engineers, town-planners, etc.) On the one hand these changes are a symptom of a certain confusion within

11   M. Abrams, 'Architects', an *Observer* Survey, 1964.

the profession and the professional body, concerning the 'true' role of the occupation, and on the other have threatened the architect's occupational role. That such changes have on the whole been contrary to the interests of architecture is also, of course, a result of the weakness of the professional body which has been relatively inadequate in providing a firm, coherent outline of the nature of the occupation, and more important, in fighting to establish an area of occupational monopoly.

It could be suggested that the R.I.B.A. has been unable, or has not attempted with sufficient vigour, to stress the social importance and sanctity of architectural work, to emphasise the mystical role of the practitioner in his monopoly of certain sorts of important and socially vital skills and knowledge, and to establish the dangers of illegitimate or unqualified intrusion into this area. Similarly, while the architects in this sample clearly agree with one of the primary defining characteristics of a profession — that they are socialised and initiated into a body of values, attitudes, skills and knowledge, into an occupational culture — they tend to have difficulty, as the findings discussed and presented so far suggest, in establishing their professional *authority,* their sphere of competence. When this occurs, it is likely to be a source of individual anxiety.

Some typical statements about architects' work frustrations and difficulties were:

> 'Oh, lots of things are (wrong with this job), red tape, petty, ridiculous bye-laws, the hours you have to spend on administrative work, the moronic clients. The only good thing about this job is when you get to the drawing board, and that's getting more and more difficult.'

> 'We're subject to a variety of absolutely maddening frustrations: clients who change their minds all the time, builders who are completely incompetent and fifty years behind the times.'

> 'It's the routine drudgery that I hate most. Sometimes I spend months doing details and I don't even know what they're going into.'

The architects, like the railwaymen, had a firm idea of their 'real' work; by it they meant that work activity which is, or should be, specific to members of their occupation and for which they have specific training and skills. As with the railwaymen, jobs were assessed and evaluated according to the opportunities they offered for this sort of work.

On the whole, however, while many architects were and had been frustrated they were still optimistic about their chances within the occupation. For most of them this optimism centred around their aspiration to become private-practice principals. With enough money they felt that they would be able to accept only those commissions which they found genuinely stimulating. Also 80.77 per cent of the architects would repeat their choice of career if they could start their career again, and 88.46 per cent would be pleased if a son of theirs wanted to become an architect. However these conclusions do not belie the earlier suggestion that the architects were worried about the organisation of their occupation and their professional role. They merely suggest that on the whole the architects still felt that the satisfactions they derived – or hoped at some future occasion to derive – from their work, overcame the annoyances and frustrations.

Conclusion
The important conclusion to be drawn from the data presented above on the architects' and railwaymen's attitudes towards and feelings about their work and jobs is that members of both samples were emotionally involved in their work skills, activities and tasks. This is shown as much by the things they found frustrating in their work as by those they found satisfying. This involvement was related to the respondents' work-based expectations and values and the historical nature of their work.

Marginality
While it appeared that members of both occupational communities were involved in their work tasks and skills, it has already been suggested that involvement alone is a necessary but not a sufficient causal factor. Certainly in the existing evidence there is no example of members of the community who are involved in their work but are not subject to at least one of the other postulated determinants. In this section the applicability of the second determinant outlined in Chapter 2 – marginality – will be investigated.

The ways in which marginality affects men's choice of leisure-time associates are clear. Members of an occupation can be said to be in a marginal situation when they want to associate with members of a higher-status group but are unable to do so. These aspirations are the result of members of the occupation 'overestimating' the status level of their occupation, for a variety of reasons; they consider their occupation to be worthy of a greater amount of social honour then other, non-members are prepared to accord them. And this 'overestimation' is displayed in terms of associational aspirations: when they find that they are unable to associate with their chosen associates they tend to retreat into their occupation and to select their friends and associates from among their occupational peers.

To what extent, if at all, were members of the two occupational samples marginal in this sense? To what extent was the preferential association the result of their being unable to associate with people of their choice?

Railwaymen

Certainly the railwaymen considered that the status position of their occupation had declined over the last thirty to forty years. This was one of the most frequent topics of conversation among the railwaymen, many of whom had personally experienced these changes. All the railwaymen in the sample had spent more than fifteen years working for the railways: 96.08 per cent had done more than twenty years and 47.06 per cent had done more than thirty. One railwayman said, echoing the sentiments of many: 'When I joined the railways, a railwayman was king of the working class; now he's a laughing stock. From top to bottom in a lifetime!'

The railwaymen's feelings about the changes in the status level of their occupation were frequently expressed in terms of certain differences that they felt existed between themselves and their contemporaries and people who were currently joining the occupation. Eighty (80.39) per cent thought that, compared with themselves and their contemporaries as recruits, the recruits of today were incompetent in technique and defective in their approach to the work. Many claimed that this was both a result of, and a reason for the reduction in the status level of the occupation.

At the time when most of the sample joined the railways it was one of the best working-class jobs available — both in economic and in status terms. Frequently the respondents described how difficult it was to get a job on the railways in their day, and their pride at being taken on. Today, it was claimed, things had changed. One driver remarked: 'When we first joined the railways forty years ago only the cream could get a job on the railways because it was the best job going. Now it's all different, now its the left-overs, the scum that joins the railways.'

The esteem in which railwaymen used to be generally held within the working class was firmly based on certain economic aspects of their work: not only was it one of the best-paid working-class jobs, it was also one of the most secure. The railwaymen stressed this security, which, they felt, made them different from others. Two remarks illustrate this:

> 'You could walk into any shop in Cambridge in them days and just order something and say, "I'm a railwayman" and walk out with it. Everyone knew it was a good job.'

> 'A man who could get a job on the railways sold his birthright away, but he knew he'd be alright for life.'

The railwaymen said two things were responsible for this decline in status level: the declining importance of the railways as a form of transport, and the decline in the relative economic position of railwaymen *vis-à-vis* other working-class jobs. It was also apparent that because of changes in the nature of railway work itself — its organisation, security and technology — the railwaymen too felt that it was very much less of a 'good' job, i.e. one that people admired and wished to have.

But the railwaymen still maintained that their work was more important, more worthy of respect and honour than was usually felt. In saying this they stressed, as members of occupations usually do when making a case for greater occupational honour, that they were providing an important public service, that this involved them in dangerous and demanding work and that they were only able and prepared to accept this responsibility because of their non-instrumental orientation towards work and work tasks. They frequently said that in this respect they differed from members of other working-class occupations who worked only for money (and who made more than they did), who took, and were capable of taking, no responsibility, and whose work was, as they saw it, meaningless, mindless and of no social value.

When railwaymen were asked to suggest other occupations that they considered to be similar to theirs, nearly half the sample 49.02 per cent compared themselves with a higher-status occupational group, often air-line pilots or air-traffic controllers. Inevitably these comparisons were justified in terms of the amount of responsibility involved and the capacity to accept responsibility ('In this game you can't throw your mistakes out and start again') which is something that the railwaymen in this sample valued most highly.

However, despite the fact that railwaymen considered that their work was no longer accorded the sort of status it deserved, and some compared it to middle-class occupations, none of them suggested that railwaymen should be accorded middle-class status or be accepted as associates of middle-class people. On the contrary they stressed and valued their membership of the working-class. Railwaymen's answers to the question on comparable occupations must be understood not in terms of their marginality but as an aspect of their constant struggle to emphasise the skill and responsibility of railway work; a struggle which they are losing and which they know they are losing.

The railwaymen were not, then, marginal: they did not have colleague friends merely because they were unable to associate with members of some high-status group. On the contrary there is evidence that railwaymen were highly committed to their own occupational value system and culture which was based on their work skills and their pride in doing their work. They did not identify with middle-class value systems. In as much as they had any desire to associate with other skilled manual workers there was no evidence that they had any difficulty in this; most of the railwaymen's non-colleague friends were other skilled workers.[12]

Architects

The architects did not feel that their occupation had undergone any marked change in status position. Most apparently felt that, overall, architecture was relatively deprived in this respect, *vis-à-vis* the other professions (and it was suggested that this was a result of the weaknesses of architecture as a profession in this country), but that some improvement was discernible. Certainly the architects felt that the public was becoming more aware of what architecture was about, and more interested in design generally. This is further demonstrated by the fact that 62.75 per cent thought that current recruits were of a higher standard than those entering the profession when they joined.

There is no evidence that architects experience any sort of blocked associational aspirations; most of their non-architect friends were other professionals or people in types of work broadly similar to their own. The fact that architects associate with each other was the result, not of a retreat into the profession in the face of extra-occupational associational difficulties, but of the degree to which architects shared a work-based culture, and an involvement in work skills, tasks and interests which they have incorporated into their view of themselves.

Inclusive Factors

The third suggested determinant of occupational communities has been called inclusive factors. These are those features of a man's job which affect his non-work life, interests and activities. Some jobs have little further influence on a man's life after the end of the working day until he returns to work the next day — or the next shift — but other jobs penetrate and influence many aspects of a man's leisure-time. Our interest in inclusive factors is mainly restricted to those that affect a man's ability to participate in non-work-based relationships, organisations and activities. Three types of inclusive factor have been isolated (see Chapter 2): organisational pervasiveness, organisational embrace and restrictive factors.

Organisational pervasiveness

The pervasiveness of an organisation means the degree to which members of an organisation share a value system, a culture which they are obliged to

12 There is no evidence that the railwaymen experience *any* associational difficulties. They were asked: 'Do you find it difficult in any way to get along with people who are not architects/railwaymen?' Ninety-two (92.16) per cent of the railwaymen said they had no difficulty of this sort. The minority who gave positive answer said that these difficulties were the result of shift work.

acquire and accept and identify with because of their membership of the organisation. Such a value system is disseminated through processes of secondary socialisation backed up by a variety of sanctions, should these be necessary In most cases of course sanctions are not necessary because as a result of their training the incumbents are thoroughly involved in the organisational culture. Selection is also important in this respect. So defined, it is clear that members of all professions are subject to organisational pervasiveness because of their participation in the professional training scheme which imparts, along with the relevant body of knowledge and expertise, a work-based, global culture.

A second type of organisational pervasiveness occurs in those situations where members of an organisation or occupation are officially subject to a formalised set of rules and procedures which derives from and is enforced by senior, authoritative groups within the organisation, and which refer to, govern or restrict outside behaviour; or, alternatively, which are so vague or general as to affect incumbents in such a total way as to influence their out-of-work activities and attitudes, willy-nilly.

Clearly the professions are examples of this sort of thing *par exellence*. As Denzin has noted:

'They (professions) recruit only certain types of persons, they develop highly elaborate ideologies and supra-individual values, they have their own mechanisms of socialisation and they often attempt to proselytise and bring new persons into the fold.' (Jackson, who quotes this excerpt, goes on to add that)

'the true "professional" is work oriented to the highest possible degree – for him it is the basis of a social movement developing, the more professionalised it is; a code of ethics and ideology comprehending not merely the work situation but extending beyond this to define a status and a style of life of universal relevance, in all aspects of life. . . For such occupations the broader aspects of a socialisation process and educational framework, which not only closely controls selection but also provides training in terms of a general tradition, are clearly particularly appropriate.'[13]

But as was shown in Chapter 3, the professions are not the only type of occupation to involve this sort of organisational control. The police, for

13   N.K. Denzin, 'Pharmacy – Incomplete Professionalisation', in *Social Forces,* vol. 46, no. 3, 1968, p. 376. Quoted in J.A. Jackson, 'Professions and Professionalisation – Editorial Introduction', in J.A. Jackson (ed.), *Professions and Professionalisation*, (Cambridge University Press, 1970), pp. 5–6.

example, are subject to rules and regulations governing their out-of-work lives and activities.[14]

Members of our two occupational samples belonged in a sense to two organisations: their employing organisation and their professional association or union. However it was only the architects who could properly be said to be subject to organisational pervasiveness. In their case it derived from their professional association in two ways. Firstly architects were subject to a professional code of conduct which was quite explicitly formulated and enforced by the architects' professional association. It is true that this code of conduct applied to relatively few matters and had considerably less bite to it than other professional codes, where the 'sacredness' of the issues concerned has been established; but nevertheless the professional code existed. Secondly, and more important, architects learnt and accepted a body of professional values, their professional culture, as they went through their professional training. It is argued that acceptance of the architects' values described in the next chapter followed from membership of the profession, and is a result of the processes necessary to obtain full, qualified membership. In this sense it can be argued that the architects' value system is 'set' by the profession.

On the other hand, the values that the railwaymen shared were not 'set' in this sense by any organisation of which they were members. Acceptance of the railwaymen's values did not follow from membership of any work organisation but from participation in the community itself. The railwaymen's occupational culture was more a *result* of their occupational community than a *determinant* of it, although admittedly this distinction is not always easy to draw, given the marked degrees of inter-dependence that occurs.

Organisational embrace
This means the attempt on the part of the organisation to 'serve as the collectivity in which many or most of an individual's activities take place.'[15]

---

14   So too, at least to some extent, are those managers who work for large corporations and companies. There is a very real sense in which it could be argued that members of large corporations tend to share values, opinions, attitudes, etc., which are considered typical of those employed – at least at a salaried level – by the corporation. However, it is doubtful if such organisational traits and values are carried out of the organisation into the outside world, except in cases of extreme conformity.

15   Etzioni, *A Comparative Analysis*, p. 160. Saying that the organisation sets values or controls incumbents' lives does not involve any reification. Of course organisations do not act; but the people in them certainly do. And it would be absurd to deny that to be a member of an organisation means that one is subject to the power of those who own and control the organisation. For some people the organisation is most definitely an external, objective, constraining influence.

Members of an organisation characterised by a high degree of organisational embrace might eat, live and work together. Examples that come immediately to mind are the armed forces, prisons, hospitals, the merchant navy and so on. Organisational embrace clearly has very great influence on men's ability to participate in non-work-based relationships, etc.

The railwaymen in the sample were not subject to this sort of organisational embrace deriving from either their employer or their union. Historically railwaymen's lives were dominated by the railways, for example they frequently lived in houses owned by the railways; but they are no longer subject to this sort of organisational control. This is not to deny of course that they associated with their work-mates outside work and chose to live within a work-dominated occupational community, but it is to suggest that, to the extent that this occurs, it is not the result of their lives being embraced by the organisation for which they work.

Architects were not subject to this sort of control either. It is not common among the professions.

Restrictive factors
Certain features of the way that a man's work is organised and carried out can seriously affect his opportunities to get to know and make friends of, people outside his occupation or work group, and can also affect his leisure-time activities and interests. Other studies have shown that these restrictive factors are particularly important in the case of occupational communities. In most cases restrictive factors refer to the temporal organisation of work, i.e. the number of hours worked, the times of work, etc. This sort of restrictive factor will receive most emphasis here.

Railwaymen
The railwaymen in the sample did not work such a *quantity* of hours that they were unable in their free time to do anything but rest and recover. Railwaymen work a minimum of a forty-hour working week, and any time over that counts as overtime; however only 15.69 per cent of the sample did more that five hours overtime in an average week, and none of them did more than ten hours.

However all the railwaymen worked shifts and had done so for as long as they had worked for the railways. In consequence they were at home, or at rest, when others were at work. The respondents were asked, 'What particular ways are there in which your work can affect your out-of-work life?' Railwaymen's answers are revealing. Ninety-eight (98.04) per cent mentioned shift work and 90.20 per cent the times when they worked.

However it is not simply the times when railwaymen work that restrict their out-of-work lives; a second factor was that for most of the railwaymen these shifts did not begin at regular, established times. Although they were given advance notice of their future working times, most knew from experience that these were, at best, approximate. Furthermore, not only were they uncertain about starting times, they couldn't be sure when they were going to finish either. Drivers were particularly subject to this type of uncertainty. One said: 'When I walk out that door the wife can't be sure when I'm coming back till she sees me come back through it. I was once twelve hours late home from work.'

Most of the railwaymen found at least some aspect of their times of work, or shift work, upsetting, inconvenient or annoying. Some found them extremely annoying while others found them merely occasionally inconvenient. When railwaymen were asked about the things they disliked about their work 52.92 per cent mentioned shift work; and among the 72.55 per cent who said that if they inherited so much money that work was no longer necessary, they would stop working or take another job, many mentioned shift work as the source of their annoyance.

It seems likely that shift work has a number of effects on railwaymen's lives. For example many of the railwaymen with small children said that shift work gave them more time at home with their families, since they had time off during the hours that their children were available. Similarly many of the respondents suggested that shift work had put a considerable strain on their wives, and their marriages. One said: 'If you want to know about the railways you should ask the wife. She's the one who has had to put up with the shift work for the last twenty five years.'

But the most obvious and important feature of shift work was the effect it had on railwaymen's ability to participate in clubs, societies and group leisure activities. Because they often worked during the evenings when group activities often take place they were unable to involve themselves in any sorts of activities which required regular attendance. One railwayman, who strongly resented this 'interference' in his non-work life, said:

'I used to be a keen cricketer, but that's over now. You can't do a thing like that when you work for the railways because I could never be there for matches. When you work for the railways you are like a slave, the railways run your life, there's no room for anything else.'

The restrictive factors to which the railwaymen were subject affected their hobbies in two ways. First, the times when railwaymen worked meant that they spent many daylight hours at home; and obviously day-light hours are particularly suitable for certain sorts of leisure activities (gardening and out-door activities), and particularly unsuitable for others (going to the cinema, or using other commercial entertainment facilities). One summed it up: 'When you're on shift work you're free when everyone's at work and you're at home when everything's closed. That's why railwaymen are so domestic around the house.'

Secondly, shift work meant that railwaymen found it difficult to take part in hobbies which need other people. Solitary activities are clearly more suitable.

Similarly the times when railwaymen worked and their uncertainty about their future working times make it difficult for them to establish and main-tain friendships with people outside their work situation, or to interact in an organised way with people outside their work.

However the fact that railwaymen found it difficult to get to know and make friends of people outside their occupation cannot explain why, as the next chapter shows, so many of them had friends from their occupation. After all it is perfectly possible for people who are subjected to restrictive factors to react by having no friends at all. Railwaymen have friends from their occu-pation because they shared their involvement in their work skills and tasks and lived in the same work-bound world. The importance of the restrictive factors lies in their effect on the *pattern* of railwaymen's preferential association. As will be seen in Chapter 5, the railwaymen in the sample were friendly with their work-mates, rather than with other members of their occupation, be-cause the times they worked made it difficult to get to know people except when they were at work.

Architects

Few if any of the architects worked so many hours that they were unable to find time to do anything else. However 78.85 per cent thought that their lives were affected in some ways by their hours or work. They mentioned having to work late, taking work home and doing rush jobs. However it is doubtful if this had a severe effect on their non-work lives as it happened only occasion-ally, and most architects have at least some flexibility in their working times.

In this chapter an attempt has been made to assess which, if any, of the suggested determinants of occupational communities outlined to Chapter 2 were operative and applicable in the cases of architects and railwaymen. It has been found that in both cases two of these determinant factors appear to be present. The next chapter will present data on the nature of the two occupational communities with a view to relating it to the different com-binations of determinants discussed above.

5

The occupational communities of architects and railwaymen

Having established that the two occupational samples were exposed to (different) combinations of the factors that are held to determine the nature and occurrence of occupational communities, it is now appropriate to present the data on the work/leisure relationships of the two occupational samples and demonstrate that variations between the samples are the result of variations in the patterns of determination. The three suggested components of occupational communities will be considered in turn.

Self-Image

Do architects and railwaymen see themselves in terms of their occupational role and/or titles, and if so, what does this mean to them? *What sort of people do they see themselves as?*

That the architects and railwaymen did see themselves in terms of their occupational title was strikingly evident; even before they were questioned on this point[1] many of the interviewees made it clear that they saw themselves as architects or railwaymen — and that this title was a source of pride and satisfaction to them. Respondents would frequently speak of 'us railwaymen' or say things like: '. . . of course the thing about us architects'. It was also apparent, without direct questioning on the point, that respondents' perceptions of themselves in terms of their occupational title carried with it a view

---

1   The first point to make on this is the remarkable difficulty of questioning people about it. Although it might seem best to simply ask respondents 'How do you see yourself?' or even more bluntly 'Who are you?', the pilot interviews showed, not surprisingly, that these questions were totally bewildering. (Although people probably do differentiate interviews — and particularly sociological research interviews — from ordinary interactions and communicative behaviour, there are limits to their flexibility and tolerance, and, indeed, their comprehension.) The question 'Who are you?' was used by Kuhn and McPartland in their investigation of self attitudes. M.H. Kuhn and Thomas S. McPartland, 'An Empirical Investigation of Self Attitudes', in *American Sociological Review,* Vol. 19, 1954, pp. 68–76.

of themselves as people with specific abilities, skills, attitudes and qualities. These will be described later.

Respondents were asked the question, 'When was it that you first saw yourself as an architect/railwayman?' (as appropriate). This question, which replaced an earlier one that was found to cause difficulties, is to some extent loaded; it makes it difficult for an interviewee to deny that he sees himself in terms of his occupational role. However, there was considerable evidence, from the pilot interviews and unstructured discussions, that the respondents did see themselves in this way, and it was still possible for them to give a negative answer.

All but eight of the architects (15.38 per cent), saw themselves in terms of their occupational title. Most of them could remember the occasion when they first made this identification: it was usually when they had completed, for the first time, what they considered to be the basic work tasks of the fully qualified professional architect, i.e. in most cases when they were first responsible for the entire design process. The architects' professional identification was contingent upon their being able to claim, with confidence, the professional autonomy which is the most important single element in their professional value system. A very small number of the architects (11.54 per cent) said that they did not see themselves in this way *yet*. They added that this was because they had not amassed enough experience to enable them to satisfy themselves of their claim to the title. This is interesting for the light it sheds on 'labelling theory'. It seems unlikely that these people, who were, for the moment anyway, *resisting* the title or label 'architect', were not called that by outsiders, possibly even by colleagues and contractors, etc. Yet far from becoming what they were called, they would not accept the title until they themselves felt that they had become architects. It would be a mistake to labour this point, for there are obviously cases where the title carries more drastic implications than this one, and where people have less chance to escape the implications of the title, because attitudes towards them are determined by it. But it does emphasise that people do tend, when they are able, to resist labelling when they think it premature, or undeserved.

Most of the architects were closely attached to their occupational role in that it was, as Goffman has said: 'One of which he may become effectively and cognitively enamoured, desiring and expecting to see himself in terms of the enactment of the role and the self-identity emerging from this enactment.'[2] However, this did not stop them — and the railwaymen on occasion — from behaving in a way which suggested that they weren't simply 'typical' architects (or railwaymen), that they were unlike the others in this or that respect, that

2   Erving Goffman, *Encounters: Two Studies in the Sociology of Interaction,* (New York, Bobbs-Merrill), 1961, p. 89.

they didn't take this as seriously as the others, and so on. These sorts of comments, which could be seen as examples of role distance, are interesting because they confirm that members of the two occupations do have a view of the typical member, his interests, predispositions and values.

Most of the architects remembered the time when they first identified themselves completely with their occupation. (They were asked 'What did this mean to you?', 'How did you feel?'.) Fifty-six per cent of them expressed their pride and satisfaction. Some typical comments were:

'I remember the occasion well, it was when I first designed and built — when I was responsible for the whole process. It was a marvellous moment'

'I was so proud that I took off like a jet.'

'It was like becoming a father.'

But a number of their answers reflected not their feelings about identification, but the content of it — *how* they then saw themselves, the qualities and interests of an architect. This was an issue that was also investigated directly with the question: 'Do you think that architects/railwaymen are in any way different from other people?' Ninety (90.38) per cent of the architects felt that members of their profession differed from outsiders in some way, and over three-quarters (76.92 per cent) thought that architects differed from outsiders in their interest in and capacity for design and aesthetic issues generally. Whatever their criteria of good design — and there can be no doubt that there was considerable variation on this — architects stressed their interest in the way things are designed; and they frequently stressed that their interest in the visual was not restricted to their work but affected their perception generally, and totally. Architects, it was frequently remarked, see things with architects' eyes. And it was claimed that their concern for design was displayed (or advertised) in their choice of possessions, furniture, clothes, etc. A number of the architects also mentioned a particular intellectual style, a sort of clarity and incisiveness, which they felt characterised members of their profession. This was related to the nature of architects' work and to the consequences of making mistakes. Confirmation of the extent to which architects see themselves as different from other people was obtained by asking them a further question: 'Do you think architects/railwaymen have similar attitudes on things generally?' Data from this question will be presented later, but at this stage it should be noted that 88.46 per cent of the architects thought they shared a common attitude or approach (including the sort of attitudes towards design etc. mentioned above).

Finally the respondents were asked: 'What are the necessary qualities of a good architect/railwayman?' The main purpose of this question was to obtain information on the occupational value systems, but it also unearthed some interesting data on their occupational identifications. For example 25.00 per cent of the architects mentioned certain personality characteristics, which it was felt were necessary, if they were to overcome the obstacles and difficulties they were likely to meet in their work. Tenacity, resilience, patience, stubbornness, courage and integrity were all mentioned. The good architect, it was felt, would need all these if he were to overcome interference from clients, commercial pressures and many other work frustrations. (Of course, predictably, considering what has gone before, the most popular characteristic of the good architect — mentioned by 88 per cent of them — was excellence of design.)

Like the architects the vast majority of the railwaymen (96.08 per cent) said that they saw themselves in terms of their occupational title and that this was a source of pride and satisfaction. Most of the railwaymen said that this first occurred when they had obtained the support and approval of their workmates, or when they had attained a rank — fireman, driver or signalman — which meant that they would have to exercise responsibility and expertise. They too were strongly attached to their occupational role. One railwayman said of the first occasion of this self-identification: 'Oh it was when I first got my uniform, after twelve months service. I remember blacking my face so that people would think I was a fireman. I was that proud to be a railwayman.' Two-thirds of the railwaymen remembered this occasion as a moment of pride and self-satisfaction, and many said that it was one of most important moments in their lives, for it meant that they had entered an elite brotherhood, that they had taken an important step in their career.[3] Some representative comments were:

'I felt as big as the Catholic Church the day I first went out on the road.'

'I felt as pleased as a dog with two tails.'

'I knew that I'd started then, that I'd made the grade.'

---

3   Sherif and Cantril describe this process, whereby men attempt to involve themselves in relationships and groups which hold values they adhere to, or are beginning to adhere to, as 'ego striving'. They write: 'Ego-striving, then, is the individual's effort to place himself in those constellations of human relationships that represent *for him* desirable values that will make *his* status or position secure.' M. Sherif and H. Cantril, *The Psychology of Ego-Involvements,* (New York, Wiley, 1947), p. 115.

Many of the railwaymen stressed that this self-identification in occupational terms was the product of long, hard-gained experience. One remarked: 'It takes time to become a railwayman. You can't learn this job from a book or from schooling, it's experience on the job that counts, and that takes years.'

I shall return later to the importance of time, of an historical perspective. It is impossible to understand the plight of railwaymen today, or their views and behaviour, unless one realises the truth of the remark – 'It takes time to become a railwayman'.

In answering the question on occupational identification nearly a quarter of the railwaymen spoke not of *how they felt* on this occasion, but of *how they saw themselves*. They listed the qualities, interests and abilities which they considered typified the railwayman. (It was remarkable how convinced the railwaymen – and the architects – were of their distinctiveness, and how much they relished discussing these differences.) Most of the characteristics mentioned concerned either the relationship between railwaymen, or the way that railwaymen see their work. In the first category were such characteristics as being helpful to one's work-mates and dealing fairly with them; in the second were such traits as conscientiousness, responsibility and taking a pride in one's work.

More information on the nature of railwaymen's self-perceived distinctiveness was obtained through the question, 'Do you think that architects/railwaymen are in any way different from other people?'. Eighty (80.39) per cent of the railwaymen said that they saw themselves as different. The difference most frequently mentioned was their capacity to accept responsibility, which was the result of the dangerous and demanding nature of their work. It was often said that railwaymen were particularly steady, reliable, trustworthy people, and it is possible that this belief is generally accepted, since retired or redundant railwaymen are often employed in jobs concerned with security.

The nature of relationships between railwaymen was often mentioned. Probably the most common of all was the often-repeated: 'We're a race apart, a different breed you know.' This saying was so common it clearly has the status of a widely held 'fact'; and there can be little doubt that it does not simply describe the way things are; it also described how things should be. This is also true of the railwaymen's comments about their attitudes towards their work: they described how they thought railwaymen *should* feel, *should* behave, not just how they did regard their work.

Railwaymen's answers to the question 'Do you think that architects/railwaymen have similar attitudes on things generally?' (as appropriate) revealed that 72.55 per cent felt that they had, and this included political views, i.e. support for the Labour Party. The 'good' railwaman is a supporter of the Labour

Party just as Cannon[4] has suggested the 'good' compositor is. It was not possible, in this research, to explore the respondents' 'political' views in any detail. But one thing certainly emerged: that it would be misleading and simplistic to consider that railwaymen's apparent loyalty to the Labour Party has any clear political meaning, or that this is all there is to the railwaymen's political attitudes. Their feelings about their own situations, experiences and disappointments — which sometimes revealed a deep and distressing bitterness — show that it is necessary to be wary of defining 'political' purely in 'party political' terms. One interesting question to ask of the railwaymen — or indeed of any occupational group whose situation has, in their view, deteriorated — is when, and under what circumstances, do members of that occupation define their deprivation as a political event. Political, in this sense, as Hindess has put it, pertains 'to the social structuring of power and its uses'.[5] And how does this sort of political awareness relate to their political activity in the usual sense of supporting, or voting for, a political party?

But although the railwaymen's support for the Labour Party cannot be taken to be the sum of their political views and attitudes — for, in reply to other questions on their feelings about their work, they revealed many more 'radical' views than the party supports — it does demonstrate the central importance, to the railwaymen, of the ideal of brotherhood. This, rather than because they believed the Labour Party represented their interests, is why they are loyal to the Party. And this ideal is, in their opinion, represented in their occupational community.

Railwaymen's answers to the question on the qualities of the good railwayman showed a remarkable unanimity — and intensity. Sixty-three (62.75) per cent mentioned proficiency at work tasks, and 72.55 per cent attitudes towards work. These were, of course, closely inter-connected. The following comments illustrate these views:

'A good railwayman knows his job from A to Z.'

'A good railwayman, a real railwayman, could do his job blindfold, and never make a mistake.'

4   I.C. Cannon, 'Ideology and Occupational Community: A Study of Compositors', in *Sociology*, vol. 1, 1967, pp. 160—87.

5   Barry Hindess, *The Decline of Working Class Politics*, (London, MacGibbon and Kee, 1971), p. 14. This book argues most convincingly that, as far as the working class is concerned, politics is no longer considered relevant to or concerned with their experiences and interests. Hence their 'apathy', so called, or their 'deviance' from expected voting and political habits.

'A real railwayman doesn't finish at the end of his shift, he finishes when he's finished the job.'

'A man that loves his work and takes a real pride in it.'

Obviously the occupational identifications of architects and railwaymen are closely related to the value systems and cultures of the two occupations. Members of both occupations saw themselves as people with certain characteristics — abilities, skills, attitudes or personality characteristics — which they considered essential attributes of members of that occupation, essential if they were to do what they thought they should be doing in the proper way. Similarly, they ascribed to themselves and others, as architects or railwaymen, attitudes towards their work and each other which they felt were desirable. The occupational identifications are also directly related to the data on the architects' and railwaymen's involvement in work tasks and skills reported in the previous chapter. In both cases it was found that the respondents experienced their jobs as disappointing and frustrating to the extent that they were denied opportunities to display and employ what they took to be their prime occupational abilities. We have now seen that the respondents consider these skills ect. not only as important and valuable elements of their self-image, but also as 'proper' features of 'good' and competent members of their occupations.

I hope this discussion reveals — what is a central theme of this book — that work is a crucial aspect of a man's life, that 'occupations and professions are among the main mediators between the individual and society',[6] is not empty rhetoric, but the only proper, useful approach to this subject. Ronald Fraser puts it well when he writes,

'Work, as has often been noted, is not only the way each of us makes a living; it is one of the principal ways in which we "make" the society we live in and which in turn "makes" us; work — the human activity of mastering and transforming the given — is (or should be) therefore one of the principal ways in which we make ourselves.'[7]

6   Elliott A. Krause, *The Sociology of Occupations*, (Boston, Little, Brown and Company, 1971), p. 1. In this book Krause argues convincingly that occupational sociology deserves a central place in the analysis of society and social change, and that it involves, and makes use of, important theoretical sociological perspectives. The perspective he uses most fruitfully is what he calls the 'conflict of interest' approach.

7   Ronald Fraser (ed.), *Work Volume 2: Twenty Personal Accounts,* (Harmondsworth, Penguin, 1969), Introduction, p.7.

90

This section should also have made it clear that the symbolic interactionist perspective is appropriate. This emphasises the ways in which a man's identity is derived from his location in the society — and particularly his place in the division of labour — and how this identity involves social categories and is dependent on the support and confirmation of certain significant others — in these cases, colleagues.

Values: Occupational Reference Groups

This book argues that the sort of extreme work/leisure relationship which is usually called an occupational community involves members of the occupation in a shared, work-based, occupational culture. This consists of values, beliefs and knowledge. Broadly speaking, this is the sort of thing that Durkheim wrote about in his *Professional Ethics and Civic Morals:*

'As professors we have duties which are not those of merchants. Those of the industrialist are quite different from those of the soldier, those of the soldier from those of the priest, and so on. . . We might say in this connection that there are as many forms of morals as there are different callings, and since, in theory each individual carries on only one calling, the result is that these different forms of morals apply to entirely different groups of individuals.'[8]

This discussion of occupational values follows Kluckhohn and others in seeing values as 'a preference which is felt and/or considered to be justified — "morally" or by reasoning or by aesthetic judgements, usually by two or three of these'. As such, operationally, values are characterised by: approval or disapproval (ought or should statements); strong emotional responses; differential effort and choices taken or rejected.[9]

Members of occupational communities, it is suggested, do not only share values. They also share beliefs (about the consequences of deviance from these values, the necessity for them, the roles of the occupation, and the service it supplies, etc.); and a body of work-based knowledge (about the organisation of their work, its techniques, history, argot, etc.).

This occupational culture, with these elements, subtly inter-related and inter-dependent, is an historical product and is acquired by members of the

8   Durkheim, *Professional Ethics,* pp. 4–5.

9   Clyde Kluckhohn, 'Values and Value-Orientations in the Theory of Action: An Exploration in Definition and Classification', in Talcott Parsons and Edward A. Shils (ed.), *Towards a General Theory of Action: Theoretical Foundations for the Social Sciences,* (New York, Harper and Row, 1962), pp. 388–433, p. 396.

occupation as they progress in their 'career'.[10] I will discuss later its relationship to occupational experience. How it relates to the processes described in the previous section should be clear: members of occupational communities see themselves in terms of the culture they derive from their occupational reference group, and their self-images are based upon the support of their occupational peers — or some of them — who function as their significant other, their 'audience'.

The value systems may be seen, at least in part, as ideological, in that they contain a view of the occupation, its role in the society, the nature of the contribution it makes to the general good, the relationship between the occupation and other related lines of work, and the conditions necessary to ensure an adequate flow of 'suitable' recruits to the occupation. The two value systems are statements of occupational interest, and are firmly rooted in the social location of the two groups, in their class position. Secondly, the two value systems may also be seen as ideological in that they supply ordered, coherent perspectives to the sorts of situations and difficulties that members of the two occupations are likely to experience. They thus supply a framework for marshalling and interpreting social situations.[11]

The data on the occupational cultures of the architects and railwaymen will be set out as follows:

(1) Do members of the two occupational samples use an occupational reference group? Do they differ in accordance with the local/cosmopolitan distinction set out earlier?

(2) What are the main elements of the two occupational cultures?

(3) Does the fact that an architect or railwayman shares an occupational culture affect his feelings for his colleagues and, if so, in what ways?

In order to collect data on respondents' reference group identifications — to see to what extent they regarded themselves and other members of their

10   This concept has been discussed in Chapter 1. It is particularly useful because it ties together 'objective' aspects of social structure and 'subjective' interpretations and identifications. It involves what Becker calls 'situational adjustment'. He writes:

> 'The person, as he moves in and out of a variety of social situations, learns the requirements of continuing in each situation and of success in it. If he has a strong desire to continue, the ability to assess accurately what is required, and can deliver the required performance, the individual turns himself into the kind of person the situation demands.' Howard Becker, 'Personal Change in Adult Life', in *Sociometry*, 1964, pp. 40–53, p. 44.

11   This view of ideology is derived from Clifford Geertz, 'Ideology as a Cultural System', in David Apter (ed.), *Ideology and Discontent*, (New York, Free Press, 1964), pp. 47–76.

92

occupation as 'we' – they were asked, early in the interview, a series of inter-related questions: 'Do you think that compared with other people you are paid enough? Who are you comparing yourself with? Who do you mean by "you"?' The first two of these questions are useful, not only because in answering them the respondent usually revealed this occupational identification, but also because I was interested in his feelings about his earnings and the sort of occupational comparisons he made. (See previous chapter.) At this stage it is respondents' answers to the last of these questions which are of particular interest; for this question probes into their occupational identification and brings to light differences in the nature of these reference group identifications.

Sixty-seven (67.31) per cent of the architects and 96.08 per cent of the railwaymen admitted to some sort of occupational identification in answering the third of the questions set out above – 'Who do you mean by "you"?'. (For purposes of comparison, material from the two occupations will be presented concurrently.) There are, however, important differences in the type of response made by members of the two occupations. Nearly two-thirds (59.62 per cent) of the architects referred to *all* members of their occupation; but this was true of only 1.96 per cent of the railwaymen. On the other hand 94.12 per cent of the railwaymen referred to members of their particular department who shared their work situation, for example, Cambridge drivers or signalmen. This type of response was not made by any of the architects (although 8.29 per cent of the architects answered the question by referring to architects in their type of work, but even this is a much broader category than those used by the railwaymen).

Respondents' answers to this question are consistent with the suggestion, set out in Chapter 2, that occupational communities in general, and the two 'putative' communities described here in particular, can be divided into two broad types; the local and the cosmopolitan. The one is based on people who interact with each other through working together, the other on the occupation as a whole.

It is appropriate at this stage to clarify what is meant by a work-mate, since this is a term that has considerable significance to the local/cosmopolitan distinction. For many of the railwaymen and a few of the architects work was actually a solitary activity, but respondents did not regard only those people who worked alongside them as their work-mates, rather they defined as a work-mate any member of their employing organisation whom they regularly met during working hours. When the term work-mate is used in this book it is used in the same way as respondents used it – to refer to fellow members of the organisation who are frequently encountered at work, sometimes actually during the execution of work tasks, but also during breaks, in the mess room before and after work, etc. Because of the way in which railwaymen's work is performed and organised, it is safe to assume that the majority of a man's work-mates will be in the same type of railway work as himself.

There is some tendency for the sorts of occupational identification to vary with the type of work situation. The architects who did not admit to an occupational identification were predominantly those who worked either for building or construction firms or other types of non-architectural organisation, or who were private-practice principals. Presumably this is because these architects are either no longer working as 'proper' architects at what is taken to be 'proper' architectural work, or because as principals of architectural practices they were so conscious of the competition that existed between members of their profession that they did not feel that the common architectural value system was sufficient to overcome the rivalry of private practice. It is indeed a highly risky business. As one principal said: 'I'm talking about me . . . Other architects are rivals. Private practice is a cut-throat business, and it's best to know it.'

It might be argued that the different patterns of response to the question on occupational identification do not reflect any differences between the two occupational communities, but merely reveal real financial differences within each occupation. For example, it is possible that Cambridge drivers or signalmen *are* less well paid than their colleagues in other areas, and that this is why they referred to Cambridge railwaymen when answering the series of questions on satisfaction with earnings which culminated in the question on occupational identifications. In fact, although railwaymen are paid a fixed weekly wage they can also obtain bonus payments; and opportunities to obtain such payments *do* vary from one area to another, depending on the length and type of run staffed by men from the depot. Consequently, railwaymen in some depots *are* better paid than in others. The point is, however, that there are also very considerable differences between the architects in the sample, yet the architects, unlike the railwaymen, did not concentrate on the differences within their occupation but on *the differences between architects and members of other professions.* In both occupations the choice of salient differences and comparisons *follows* the initial involvement in an occupationally based reference group.

In this book the concept of reference group is being used in the normative sense: as a source of values and perspectives. This usage incorporates the idea of identification with similar others — in this case other architects and other Cambridge railwaymen — and also leads to another, related idea, that of the relativity of social comparisons. As architects and railwaymen share a work-based culture with their colleagues, or some of them, and identify with these colleagues and consider themselves, in some contexts at least, as 'we', they will therefore make certain sorts of comparisons with selected outsiders. The choice of comparison will depend on a number of variables, particularly the aspects of their work and work skills, etc., which they consider particularly important, and the nature of their actual work market and status situations.

What exactly are the work-based cultures that members of these two occupations share? Because of the nature of this research, and the constraints of time and money, it was not possible to make a thorough analysis of the two occupational cultures, and the material gathered is inevitably rather general in character; nevertheless a considerable amount of data were collected in the course of the empirical investigation, some of which has already been presented in the previous section.

It has been noted that when a group develops a value system, it will tend to be related to the shared activities and problems of the group members. Sherif and Sherif say:

> 'A code or set of values peculiar to the particular formation, in addition to what group members may share in other respects with other people of the community, is an essential produce of group formation . . . The consequential norms pertain to spheres of activity related to motives and goals that were conducive initially to frequent give and take among members.[12]

But at the same time the argument that men's ideas tend to be firmly related to the social situation, and particularly their location in the socially organised division of labour, must not be taken to mean that these ideas are some sort of *reflection* of this position. After all, what constitutes a problem for medical students, architects, or whatever, is so only because they have certain ideas and expectations of what they should be doing, and why they should be doing it. Interests themselves are part of value systems. As Harris puts it:

> 'It is not the case that in the beginning there were purposes, and men created ideologies to relate those purposes to the world they faced. Rather does the definition of purpose arise during men's exploration of the world; they locate what purposes they should pursue, just as they discover what their interests are, at the same time as they learn more about the world in trying to overcome specific problems.'[13]

12   M. Sherif and C.W. Sherif, *Reference Groups: Exploration into Conformity and Deviation of Adolescents*, (New York, Harper and Row, 1964), pp. 53–4.

13   Nigel Harris, *Beliefs in Society: The Problem of Ideology*, (Harmondsworth, Penguin, 1971), p. 27.

There is thus an intricate and subtle inter-relationship between men's ideas and their actual situations; the constraints and restrictions within which they operate and attempt to realise or maintain their occupational interests as they see them. And ideologies develop, or are received, in order to explain, to make meaningful, and to minimise, the divergence between social situations and previous ideologies.

The architects

As we have seen from the previous section 90.38 per cent of the architects thought that members of their occupation were different from other people and the majority of them thought that this difference was, broadly speaking, a difference in values and interests. Furthermore 92.31 per cent of the architects thought that members of their occupation held certain attitudes in common. Even those who were unwilling to admit that members of their occupation shared values actually applied these values when discussing the qualities of a good architect.

The architects not only shared a work-based culture: they were also subject to a formal professional code which was enforced by their professional association and which was concerned with controlling their professional behaviour in certain ways.

It has been suggested[14] that the formal professional code is necessary because the professional is in a position to exploit his client. This situation is exploitative, firstly because the problems brought to the professional are normally those which the professional alone can solve and which are beyond the client's control, and secondly because once the work is done only the professional is competent to judge it. Or so, at least, runs one view of the professions. However, it could equally well be argued that the professions are really the same as other occupational groups — seeking to protect their interests and their status by emphasising the value of their work and the importance of allowing them to control it. Indeed in these terms one distinguishing feature of professions is their success in disseminating their professional ideology throughout society[15] and in obtaining legal backing for their monopoly. The idea of service rather than financial gain, emphasised so much by professionals and most sociologists who have written on the

---

14   Goode, 'Community within a Community'.

15   For an enlargement of this idea see Vernon Dibble, 'Occupations and Ideologies', in *American Journal of Sociology*, vol. 68, 1962, pp. 229–41. This article enquires into 'the conditions under which consensus will or will not ensue from acceptance by some groups of beliefs which had emerged out of the conditions peculiar to other groups'. (p. 229).

professions, might be seen as merely a part of the public relations of the professions.[16] This point is made very forcibly by Krause, who asserts:

'When an occupation attempts to advance its interests in the society, it almost never admits that this is what is taking place. Instead, claims are made that greater power for the group is "in the public interest" . . .'

'The public interest is defined by the groups with the power to define it, and by the groups which accept such definitions by default. To define the public interest as the same as the interest of one's group is a privilege of power.[17]

One of the complaints frequently voiced by the architects in this sample was that, as a profession, they lacked this sort of power; that increasingly they saw their interests and areas of activity infiltrated, taken over, and finally dominated by other occupational groups. This point of view is nicely expressed by an architect, not in our sample, writing in Ronald Fraser's *Work Volume Two*. He writes:

'Whereas the B.M.A. is both mouthpiece and trade union to the doctor, the R.I.B.A. is neither to the architect. Were architects to strike tomorrow, little if anything would be affected. This is a sobering thought. Not only has the R.I.B.A. failed to represent architects properly, it has actually abrogated the real role they should be playing today – that of town planning – to another body, thus ensuring the eventual passing of the profession into limbo.[18]

Architecture differs from other professions too, in that as a result of the weakness of the profession and the professional body, and the *nature* of the service it offers, the client, at least in this country, feels that he has some right to control the architect's professional performance and to judge the finished product. The architects in the sample often complained that their clients were not prepared to respect their professional advice, and that they

16 And as a method of raising, or attempting to maintain, the status of the profession (or to make an occupation into a profession). For an empirical discussion of the former situation, see R.L. Simpson and Ida H. Simpson, 'The Psychiatric Attendant, Development of an Occupational Self Image in a Low Status Occupation', in *American Sociological Review*, vol. 24, 1959, pp. 389–92. It has, of course, been noted that sacrifice of short-term gains and overt exploitation could produce an increase in long-term rewards.

17 Krause, *The Sociology of Occupations*, pp. 91 and 98.

18 Christopher Gotch, 'The Architect', in Fraser (ed.), *Work Volume 2*, p. 154.

frequently attempted to interfere in their professional work. But what is the architect's 'proper' work? Many of the sample suggested that they felt uncertain about the role of the architect in modern industrial society. The growth of town planning as a separate activity, the development of new building techniques, and new design methods, as well as changes in the organisation of architectural work, all cause the architect to question his own role, as distinct from other sorts of building/design specialists. Certainly the old-fashioned notion of the architect as artist is infirm, if not actually dead.

But a large proportion of the architects in the sample still thought that in general terms the job of the architect is to design buildings. They saw themselves, and their colleagues, in terms of their design achievements. (They were however, extremely guarded about what constituted good design, and unwilling to discuss exactly what this concern with design actually meant as a day-to-day activity.) This emphasis on the design function has, of course, been noted before. It has also been noted, implicitly at least, in the previous section, where architects' feelings about the involvement in their work and their jobs was discussed. It was seen that 64 per cent mentioned 'creativity of work, the opportunity to use design skills', as sources of intrinsic satisfaction in their work. But at the same time 72 per cent mentioned factors which frustrate these opportunities as sources of work dissatisfaction.

The architects seemed to regard it as axiomatic that, given their interest in and concern for designing buildings, and since, by their reckoning, this is an artistic activity, then by virtue of the sorts of attitudes about artistic activities current in this sort of society, *they must be as free as possible from any sort of interference or restriction.* Few subjects were accorded more emphasis by the architects. In fact, of course, all architecture is limited at least by site conditions, the state of technology, and usually, financial restrictions; but architects are prepared for these. There are others that they find harder to take. Chief among these, apparently, is interference from the client. Carr-Saunders has made the point that 'Architecture differs from every other profession . . . in that the technique contains an aesthetic element.'[19]

Perhaps he should have said that its practitioners would *like* it to contain an aesthetic element, but his point remains valid: that architects are, by virtue of this concern for aesthetics, subject to the sorts of frustration common among other artists. Most of the architects said that they experienced frustrations in this area; like jazz musicians, artists and others, they frequently found that their desire for autonomy clashed with financial survival. And for those lucky enough to be in private practice the trouble came in the form of clients

19   A.M. Carr-Saunders and P.A. Wilson, *The Professions,* (Oxford University Press, 1933), p. 184.

who attempted to control the architect's artistic sensibility. The dilemma this produces has been described by Barrington Kaye: 'The architect may either insist on following the dictates of his "artistic insight" and risk losing his client, or he may keep his client by making the alterations demanded, and thereby lose his artistic autonomy.'[20]

This problem would perhaps be solved if the architect were to abandon all involvement in the artistic aspects of his role and concentrate on the technological, engineering elements. (This is dangerous in that it would then be rather difficult to separate the architect as a discrete specialist from other, related occupations.) In fact, of course, the difference between the 'artist' and the 'professional' is one of degree – and opportunity. But there were some architects in the sample who apparently felt that the important quality of the good architect was that he had satisfied the client. In terms of the more usual responses, this can probably be seen as something of a 'deviant' response.

Interference from clients is just one of a number of design obstacles which the architects had to face. For many of the architects frustrations came not from interference in their work autonomy, but from lack of any opportunity to design. Some architects worked in offices where they felt they were unable, or not permitted, to do any designing at all. The architect's work satisfactions and frustrations were discussed more fully in the previous chapter; at this stage it remains to emphasise that they evaluate their work according to the degree of design autonomy.

Because of the value architects attach to design autonomy they tended to evaluate types of architectural work in terms of the opportunities they provided for the employment of their design skills. It was generally considered that the self-employed principal of a private practice had the best chance of doing the kind of work that the architects in the sample aspired to. Although principals were especially likely to have interfering clients, at least, it was suggested, they get the chance to design complete projects which is not true for all architects. (There is also the recurring architect's dream that he might stumble upon a client of enormous wealth and sensibility; or that he might establish such a reputation that he could pick his clients and his commissions.)

The architects' aspirations to private-practice work are revealed in their answers (set out in table 5.1) to the question: 'What would you do if you won or inherited so much money that you no longer need work?'.

The vast proportion of principals would, in this hypothetical situation, remain in their present type of work. Many of them said that under these

---

20   Barrington Kaye, *The Development of the Architectural Profession in Britain. A Sociological Study*, (London, Allen and Unwin, 1960), p. 29.

Table 5.1 *Relationship between type of employment situation and anticipated reaction to obtaining so much money that work was no longer necessary*

| | Type of employment situation | |
	Principals ($n = 12$)	Non-principals* ($n = 40$)
Type of reaction	Percentage	
Would stay in present type of work	83.33	*17.95*
Would change to other type of employment (within architecture)	*16.67*	82.05

* The category 'non-principals' is composed of architects who work for building or construction firms or other non-architectural organisations and those who are employed in private practices or local authority offices.

Percentages in italic are based on numbers of ten or less.

conditions they would be able to enjoy their work all the more, for they would be able to choose their work. Most of those architects who were not principals would change their type of work under these hypothetical circumstances; and they all said that they would set up their own practices. Many added that this was a real, personal ambition which they hoped to fulfil in the future. And it seems sensible to interpret these reactions in terms of architects' desire to free themselves from the sorts of frustration mentioned in Chapter 4.

Many of the architects, when discussing the characteristics of members of their profession, mentioned that, in their view, architects shared a particular approach to the world or a world-view. Some typical remarks illustrate this:

'Architects just have their own way of looking at things.'

'Architects, unlike other people, are really aware of their environment; they really see things around them.'

'We are interested in how things work and what they look like; that's what architecture is all about; architects notice the way things are designed and made.'

Although, generally speaking, the architects saw their professional role as supplying functional works of art, many of them also stressed the social aspects of their work and used this to claim higher professional status. These architects felt that when they designed buildings they had an opportunity to affect and mould the lives of those who lived within them. Some of them spoke of producing structures which would permit and encourage the full development of the inhabitants' personalities. This aspect of architects' culture has recently been discussed critically by Alan Lipman.[21]

One interesting consequence of the fact that architects shared an occupational culture, and identified themselves with their occupational colleagues, was that they thought they would be able to identify another member of their profession even when he was personally unknown to them. Respondents were asked the following question: 'If you went to a party where you knew there were other architects/railwaymen present, but you had not met them before, would you be able to spot them without being told who they were?' Remarkably a number of the architects (59.62 per cent) thought they would be able to identify other unknown architects. Many of them added that they had once made such an identification, apparently identifying them by their clothes. Architects saw themselves as affecting a particular and distinctive clothing style. The usual elements are: bow-tie, coloured shirt, grey suit, bright socks, suede shoes or boots. Others found the exact clues they worked on more difficult to pin down. One remarked: 'Oh yes, I could spot an architect anywhere. There's just something about them. It's impossible to explain; somehow one just knows.'

It was noted in the previous chapter that architects, unlike railwaymen, are exposed to a professional value system and code of conduct which, in its official form, acts as a (relatively mild) form of control, but which as a more general professional world-view (containing conceptions of the nature of the occupation, its members, its clients, etc.) is picked up as architects undergo their professional training and socialisation. It is as a result of this socialisation into the architectural culture that architects share conceptions of the world, their work and architectural practitioners. However, this professional culture differs from the railwaymen's culture not only in that it is more elaborate and far-reaching and to some extent finds official support and expression through the professional association and its attendant literature, but also in the mechanisms whereby it is picked up and learnt. Whereas the railwaymen are exposed to and learn about the railwaymen's values *through their work,* and thus through their work-mates, the architects learn about their occupational culture during their involvement in formal processes of professional training with other persons who will become fellow members of the profession, but are unlikely to become their work-mates.

21   Alan Lipman, 'The Architectural Belief System and Social Behaviour', *British Journal of Sociology,* vol. 20, 1969, pp. 190–204.

The railwaymen

Like the architects, the railwaymen in the sample had a well-developed occupational culture; 80.39 per cent of the sample thought that members of their occupation were different from other people, and 72.55 per cent thought they held attitudes in common. Not surprisingly the subject on which they displayed this consensus was work. Among other things railwaymen stressed the skills that their work required, the 'proper' orientation that it demanded and the sort of personality characteristics that were necessary to do the job well.

Railwaymen frequently stressed that their work required intelligence and learning. One driver said: 'Being a driver is a life-long apprenticeship, you're always learning. The job demands it.' This point is repeated by another railwayman, not of our sample, who writes:

> 'We worked the heavy, dirty coal trains from the Fife pits to the yards ... The work was very unromantic, but it called for a high degree of skill; that kind of skill and knowledge that could not be picked up from textbooks or learned in colleges, but could only be acquired by years of experience on the job.'[22]

Many of the railwaymen mentioned that steam engines required a higher degree of skill than diesel; a number bitterly regretted the decline of steam power on the railways.

Many of the railwaymen mentioned the many rules and regulations, techniques, procedures, routes, etc., which must be learnt. A typical comment: 'You've got to be on top of your work all the time, there's no time to stop and ask advice.'

The railwaymen not only felt their jobs demanded a high degree of skill and expertise, they also valued these skills and abilities. Railwaymen who were particularly knowledgeable or skilled, senior men or those who had especially responsible jobs were regarded, within the community, as men of high prestige, as 'real' railwaymen. The accumulation of work-based knowledge and information, the mastery of skills and techniques, was a valued activity among the railwaymen. Once again this is clearly related to the data presented in the previous chapter, where it was argued that railwaymen derive enjoyment from actually doing their work (although of course they are likely to experience frustration in as much as they are unable to do what they think they ought to be doing in the way that they ought to be doing it).

22   Robert Bonnar, 'Negotiating at the Top', in Fraser (ed.), *Work Volume 2*, pp. 330–45, pp. 330–1.

The railwaymen considered that certain personality characteristics were essential to the good railwayman: ability to accept responsibility was frequently mentioned. This, it was asserted, was because of the nature of railway work. One signalman said: 'My work is a life and death business. I just can't throw out my mistakes and start again. I have to be right every time.' The respondents felt that they *must* be thorough and conscientious, for 'A sloppy job can kill people in this business.'

A further work-based value held by the railwaymen, and one that is closely related to their valued sense of responsibility, is the emphasis they placed on a vocational, non-instrumental attitude towards work. Many of the railwaymen stressed that the good railwayman did not do his work just for his weekly wage; he did it because he took a pride in it, for the satisfaction of a job well done. A further element in this attitude towards work is the value railwaymen place on punctuality. Cottrell has discussed the value that American railwaymen place on punctuality, and his comments seem equally valid in this century.[23] Many of the respondents boasted that they had never been late for work, or missed a day's work. One of the railwaymen in the sample had just returned from an emergency visit to the dentist where he had had all his teeth extracted. The interview had to be postponed because his replies were unintelligible, but his wife emphasised that he would go to work that afternoon as usual. She said 'He never misses a day's work, and he's never been late for work in his life.' Her husband signalled his agreement.

The good railwayman then is always punctual, reliable and steady. But many respondents felt that some of the current recruits were below standard because they did not seem to value the things that the older man did. The newcomers were not concerned with technical knowledge, they were less responsible, they saw their work merely as a means of making money. As one driver put it, 'It's the couldn't-care-less business these days.'

The railwaymen not only had strong views about how their work *should* be done, they also had attitudes about the relationship between their occupation and the larger society. They felt they supplied an important (and, previously, a glamorous) social service. As with the architects, this service aspect, and the high level of skill and conscientiousness it demands, were used as the basis for demanding higher status for the occupation — or bemoaning its decline in status.

As I have already mentioned, railwaymen place great emphasis on brotherhood. Thirty-one per cent of the sample thought that members of the

23   W.F. Cottrell, *The Railroader* (Stanford University Press, 1940).

occupation differed from outsiders because of the close, friendly relationships that exist between them, and the co-operative attitude they take towards each other. (As was noted earlier, such personality characteristics as helpfulness, trustworthiness, etc., were frequently seen as typical of railwaymen.) It was evident that railwaymen thought they *should* be friendly with each other.

The existence of Mutual Improvement Classes gave institutional form to this feeling. These classes were organised and administered by older, more experienced railwaymen to help the younger ones get through the promotion examinations. Those who ran the classes were not paid.

Once again, the railwaymen's feelings of solidarity with their occupational colleagues were, like the architects', so intense that a large proportion of them (62.75 per cent) felt they could identify other members of their occupation who were personally unknown to them. Many of them claimed to have made such an identification.

To conclude this section on the occupation cultures of the architects and railwaymen: both samples identified themselves in terms of their membership of occupationally based normative reference groups. But with architects the reference group was a cosmopolitan one composed of all members of the occupation, while with the railwaymen the occupational reference group was decidedly local, in that it was composed of people who worked with the respondent and with whom he interacted at work, who shared his work situation. Both samples shared work-based cultures which, not surprisingly, were centrally concerned with the work they did, the conditions under which they *ought* to do it (architects), the qualities and skills they ought to have and be free to use, the proper way in which they should carry out their work (railwaymen), and the sort of contribution they made to the society and the general good. Clearly these cultures can be seen to some extent as ideological, in that they are statements of the interests of members of the two occupations. As a result of their shared commitment to an occupational culture, members of both occupations experienced feelings of solidarity and similitude with their occupational colleagues, even to the extent of feeling that they could identify other, unknown, members of their occupation.

Associations: Convergence of Work and Non-Work Activities, Interests and Relationships

The most striking aspect of the convergence of work and non-work displayed by the architects and railwaymen — and frequently noted among members of other occupational communities — was the extent to which they choose their friends and associates from among their occupational colleagues — or some of them. It was argued, in Chapter 2, that patterns of preferential association may differ: they may have a local or a cosmopolitan basis. This distinction was investigated with reference to the two occupational samples. (It was suggested that members of local communities would be friends with work-*mates;* members of cosmopolitan communities would be friendly with occupational colleagues who did not necessarily work with them.)

Respondents were asked to give the occupation of their five best friends.[24] Some respondents felt that they didn't have that many friends; and in such cases they were asked how many they did have. The results are set out in table 5.2 below. This table shows that 33.33 per cent of the railwaymen, as against 1.92 per cent of the architects, had less than five best friends. The railwaymen saw very definite and distinct differences between best friends and other associates, and invested the best-friend relationship with an almost sacred significance. Architects on the other hand had no difficulty in naming their five best friends.

The extent of preferential association within the two occupational samples is displayed in table 5.3.[25]

Two points arise from this table; first, while 19.23 per cent of the architects had no architect best friends, these respondents did have other, non-architect best friends; but most of the railwaymen who had no railwaymen friends had *no best friends at all.* Secondly, 65.39 per cent of the architects and 70.59 per cent of the railwaymen had two or more best friends from their occupation. This incidence of preferential association is remarkably high, particularly when compared with most manual occupations but also when compared with high-status, middle-class occupations. Gerstl's figures, which display the variation in preferential association within high-status occupations, are set out in table 5.4.

---

24   Occasionally this question caused difficulties, because of the emotional implications of the term 'best friend' and the lack of general agreement about the meaning of the term. It is obviously a concept that many of the respondents had considered previously. When respondents had difficulty they were asked for the occupations of the five people they knew best outside their family. It was felt that some limit on numbers was necessary in order to be able to compare the responses. Other studies of friendship patterns had run into difficulties because the investigators did not know the total number of respondents' friends with whom they were dealing. See Mott *et al., Shift Work,* especially p. 21.

25   Friendship patterns are regarded as a central element in an occupational community. The number of friendships investigated was limited for strategic reasons; in discussions of these data the *proportion* of a man's friends who are in the same occupation will be stressed. It will be assumed that all respondents had five best friends. This is because any other system could be misleading. If a man has only one friend and he is from the same occupation, then strictly speaking 100 per cent of his best friends are colleagues. This gives a mistaken impression of his participation in the occupational community.

Table 5.2 *Number of best friends, up to a maximum of five*

Number of best friends	Architects (n = 52) Percentage	Railwaymen (n = 51)
0	–	9.80
1	–	5.88
2	1.92	–
3	–	11.76
4	–	5.88
5	98.08	66.67

Table 5.3 *Number of best friends in the same occupation*

Number of colleague friends	Architects (n = 52) Percentage	Railwaymen (n = 51)
0	19.23	3.92
1	15.38	15.69
2	40.38	15.69
3	17.31	29.41
4	5.77	13.73
5	1.92	11.76
D.N.A.*	–	9.80

* This category is for those respondents who had no best friends,

Table 5.4 *Inclusion of colleagues among ten best friends by occupation*

Proportion of colleagues	Admen	Dentists	Professors
Low	36%	80%	12%
High	64%	20%	88%
Total	100%	100%	100%
No. of cases	(25)	(25)	(25)

Proportion dichotomised at one-fourth. Source: Joel. E. Gerstl, 'Determinants of Occupational Community in High Status Occupations.'

Respondents were actually asked the occupations of their five best friends, not how many were in the same occupation. This was done in order to avoid bias in their answers and also in order to obtain data on respondents' friendship patterns in their entirety. The most interesting additional information thus gained concern architects' friendships with people in related work. These data are presented in table 5.5

Table 5.5 *Number of best friends in related occupations (architects only)*

Number of friends in related work	Architects (n = 52) Percentage
0	38.46
1	40.38
2	17.31
3	3.85
4	100

Related occupations, in this context, means such things as town-planners, artists, engineers, surveyors, designers.

This table shows that 61.54 per cent of the architects had at least one friend from a related occupation. Architects who work for building or construction firms, or for other types of non-architectural organisations, and architects who were private-practice principals, were more likely than architects who worked in private or authority offices to have friends from occupations related to architecture, and less likely to have friends from the occupation itself. This is most marked among private-practice principals, only 16.67 per cent of whom had two or more architect friends (as against 65.39 per cent of the sample as a whole), and is probably the result of the sort of competitor/colleague relationships in which they were involved. As one principal said: 'You can't be too friendly with other architects because either you are envious of his business, or he's envious of yours.'

Principals also have to spend a great deal of their time trying to drum up business, and so preferred not to waste their time with other architects who were not going to be of any use in this respect.

During the pilot interviews a number of respondents from both occupations stressed the distinction — for them — between 'best friends' and 'associates', or 'acquaintances'. It was clear that these terms described very different sorts of relationships and consequently, during the interview proper, respondents were asked who they met frequently. They were asked: 'Do you meet other architects or railwaymen casually — at lunchtime, in the evening, or just in the street?' Eighty-one (80.77) per cent of the architects and seventy-six (76.47) per cent of the railwaymen said that they did meet their work or occupational colleagues 'regularly' or 'occasionally'.

Architects who associated casually with their colleagues said that this association usually took place during their lunchtimes or in the evening after work. Railwaymen said that such association usually took place in the vicinity of their home. Many made remarks like the following:

'You can't walk down the street without meeting another railwayman.'

'There's lots of railwaymen around here — you couldn't avoid them if you wanted to.'

Railwaymen's friends from the same occupation were nearly always their work-mates (90.20 per cent) as defined earlier, but this was less true of architects, only 23.08 per cent of whose colleague friends were work-mates. These differences in patterns of preferential association between the two occupational samples reflect the differences in occupational reference group identification discussed earlier.

The different structures of the two occupational communities are related to the different patterns of intra-occupational mobility experienced by architects and railwaymen: 94.12 per cent of the railwaymen in the sample had always been in the type of railway work they were doing when they were interviewed, and 90.20 per cent had always worked for the Cambridge Depot. On the other hand the architects had experienced much greater occupational and geographical mobility; only 59.92 per cent had *always* been in the type of work they were in when they were interviewed, 23.08 per cent had spent *most* of their time in other sorts of architectural work, and 25.00 per cent had spent some time working outside London. Many of the architects' occupational friendships were with people who had been work-mates in previous jobs, and, all in all, 69.23 per cent of the architects' architect friends were work-mates, or had been earlier.

These differences in the pattern of preferential association displayed by the members of the two occupational samples are the result of the differences in the causal mechanisms that are present in the two cases. In Chapter 4 it was argued that whereas both samples were heavily involved in their work tasks and skills, and that this constituted a necessary determinant of respondent motivation to associate with other members of their occupation, the samples differed with respect to the 'second' determinant. In the case of the architects the other factor was that they were all involved in and committed to a professional value system and world view which derived from the profession as a whole and which the architects learnt about and accepted as they experienced their professional training and socialisation. As a result of this they identified with the occupation and profession as a whole, and in consequence their occupational friends were drawn from a much wider population (the whole occupation) than were the railwaymen's. Some evidence for this is supplied by the fact that nearly half (42.31 per cent) the architects' colleagues friends were people they had met during their training period. Of course they had often also worked with them at some time later in their careers.

It is argued, then, that the fact that the architects' colleagues friends were less frequently current (or even past) work-mates derives not only from the greater occupational mobility of architects, compared to railwaymen, but also from the fact that architects are exposed to a lengthy training and socialisation in a profession-wide architectural world-view and value system. As a result of this training experience and the value system itself they are likely to pick their colleague friends not merely from their work-mates, but from the profession as a whole.

In the case of the railwaymen, on the other hand, it is argued that, although motivated to associate with their colleagues, their work-based friendship choices are severely limited by the involvement in what were termed restrictive factors. The way their work was organised simply made it difficult if not impossible for them to get to know any colleagues other than those they met at work, or worked with. As a result their occupational community was local, i.e. made up of work-mates.

Because of the obvious importance of this suggested relationship between differences in the architects' and railwaymen's patterns of preferential association and the sorts of factors that are held to be determinants that are present in the two cases, it is necessary to consider the possibility that the differences in type of preferential association, indeed the classification of the two communities as local and cosmopolitan, is merely an artefact of the way in which the populations were selected and limited.

Clearly there are some differences between the two samples that could be held to be relevant. For example, the architects worked in numerous organisations and all the railwaymen worked for the same organisation. Therefore it might be suggested that the railwaymen had many work-mates so it was easy to have work-mate friends, or indeed that all Cambridge railwaymen were work-mates for each other. It should be clear, however, that in terms of the way in which the concept work-mate is used in this study such suggestions are invalid. The railwaymen did not have many work-mates: they saw and interacted with relatively few people when they were at work, yet they limited their occupational friendship choices to these colleagues. The architects, of course, worked in offices and organisations of differing sizes, yet few worked on their own in the way that, say, a signalman or guard did.

Another possibility is that the differences between the two communities may stem from the residential habits of members of the two samples. Maybe architects live near other (non-work-mate) architects, and get to know them this way. This seems rather unlikely in London. But, as will be seen, it is the railwaymen who tend to live together, not the architects, and yet even so the railwaymen were friendly with railwaymen with whom they worked, rather than railwaymen who were neighbours, although sometimes these two roles coincided.

The Convergence of Work and Non-Work Activities and Interests

The convergence of friend and colleague relationships is one aspect – and the most important one – of a general convergence of work and non-work life which is a central feature of occupational communities. For members of occupational communities work is a 'central life interest'. Indeed in some cases the distinction between work and non-work is not a meaningful one. Respondents were asked a series of questions which were designed to elicit data on their non-work activities and interests. In the first of these they were offered four statements, each of which represented a sort of work/leisure relationship, and were asked to choose one which best reflected their own assessment of this relationship. Their answers are set out in table 5.6.

Table 5.6 *Assessment of the relationship between work and leisure*

	Architects ($n = 52$)	Railwaymen ($n = 51$)
'I am so involved in my work that it is often hard to say where work ends and leisure begins.'	38.46	–
'I put up with work largely because of the money, and need my leisure to recover from work.'	–	3.92
'Leisure and family are more important to me than work. I try and forget all about it in my spare time.'	1.92	15.69
'A man can only really enjoy his leisure time if he gets something other than just money out of his work.'	59.62	80.39

This table illustrates that the majority of the respondents felt that work and non-work were positively connected in some way. And this connection is further illustrated by the fact that members of both samples were prepared and eager to think and talk about their work and their careers in their free time. Three-quarters of the architects (75.00 per cent) said that they were neither able nor willing to forget about their work in their free time. One said: 'I can't stop thinking about work. This is not a nine to five job, you just can't cut it off, it's with you all the time.' Another remarked: 'If something is important to you and you are totally involved in it, how can you possibly forget about it merely because you leave the office?' The railwaymen too were very eager to talk about their work outside working hours. One railwayman's wife said:

'It's railways, railways, railways with him. All railwaymen are like it, they just want to get together and talk railways. As though they didn't have enough. If you want to find out about the railways ask the wives. We're the ones who have had the railways all these years.'

Not only did many of the respondents think and talk about their work during their non-work time, but many of them were also members of societies, clubs, and other types of voluntary association which were in some way connected with their work. Thirty-nine (39.22) per cent of the railwaymen and 44.23 per cent of the architects were members of some sort of work-based voluntary organisation. All were active members. Architects were members of the following semi-professional bodies: the Town Planning Institute, the Architectural Association, the Architects in Industry group, and the Association of Official Architects. They were all members of the R.I.B.A. Seventy-five (75.00) per cent had attended during the previous year. Railwaymen were members of the Railways social club or the labour club. The former was actually organised and run by British Railways Board, the latter was a well-known railwayman's haunt. All the railwaymen in the sample were members of one or another of the main railway unions. Nearly forty (39.22) per cent had attended a meeting in the previous year.

Further indication of the convergence of respondents' work and non-work lives can be obtained from a study of their hobbies. Many had hobbies which reflected their work interest, or which derived in some way from their work or the meaning it had for them. Sixty-two (61.54) per cent of the architects and 7.84 per cent of the railwaymen had work-connected hobbies, i.e. hobbies which reflected the man's interest in his work skills and tasks. Nineteen (19.23) per cent of the architects said that their main hobby was their work. By this they meant both that they regarded their work as more than just a job, and that they spent some of their leisure time in architectural work of some sort —

studying architecture and looking at buildings. Twenty-seven (26.92) per cent had artistic hobbies such as sketching, sculpturing, or designing generally. A further 15.38 per cent had such interests as modernising and converting old houses.

Few railwaymen had hobbies which could be described as work-connected in this sense. But 76.47 per cent of the sample had hobbies which were connected with the community, in that the hobby was typical of members of the railwaymen's occupational community. The main hobby was gardening. Now an interest in gardening does not derive from involvement in work skills and tasks, but from involvement in the occupational group. A large number of the railwaymen in the sample were keen gardeners; they were eager to talk about their hobby, at length, with colleagues, friends and others. It is suggested that because of the popularity of this activity among the railwaymen the hobby can be seen as a characteristic of the occupational community. (Although there are certain features of gardening as a hobby that make it particularly suited to railwaymen.)

It is felt that this remarkable convergence of work and leisure interests and activities reflects the respondents' involvement in their work, noted in the previous chapter. It is interesting that a large number of railwaymen had hobbies which they pursued with a remarkable intensity and within which they had achieved striking success. Some bred and raced pigeons, others made wine, a number were proficient automobile engineers, other played musical instruments, and so on. The railwaymen themselves frequently suggested that this was due to a sort of displacement process: in their leisure time railwaymen used neglected skills and aptitudes and fulfilled creative needs which they could not exploit at work but which their earlier work experiences had taught them to value and expect.

A final indicator of the close links that exist between the architects' and railwaymen's work and non-work lives is their preparedness to read about their work in their free time. Respondents were asked how many hours — in an average week — they spent in work-connected reading. Their answers are set out in table 5.7.

The railwaymen's work-connected reading consisted of books of regulations, new appendices to the rules, and technical works on diesel engines. Many of them pointed out the need to read regularly and reread the rule books and instructions on the many types of diesel locomotives.

Architects tend to more general reading: journals, architectural history, etc.

On the basis of the data discussed in this chapter reference to the architects' and railwaymen's *occupational communities* is justified and in view of the different patterns of preferential association and occupational reference group

112

Table 5.7 *Number of hours – in an average week – spent in work-connected reading*

Number of hours	Architects (n = 52) Percentage	Railwaymen (n = 51)
0	3.85	21.57
1	13.46	52.94
2	26.92	13.73
3	9.62	5.88
More than 3	46.15	5.88

affiliations there is reason to describe these communities as *local* and *cosmopolitan*. The two communities also differed in other ways. The railwaymen's occupational community displayed the characteristics of the 'traditional community', i.e. definite geographical boundary, multiple role relationships and connected friendship networks.

It is not surprising that the architects' community was very much less geographically based than the railwaymen's. Although 73.08 per cent of the architects' friends lived and worked within the London area, 100 per cent of the railwaymen's colleague friends lived and worked in Cambridge. Similarly the architects were not located within any particular part of North West London, while many of the railwaymen lived within a particular part of Cambridge – Romsey Town. This part of Cambridge served as a focal point for the railwaymen's occupational community.

A further difference is that railwaymen frequently had relatives and friends who were colleagues, and neighbours who were members of the same occupation as well. The architects' occupational community involved the convergence of friendship and colleague relationships, the railwaymen's community was characterised by multiple role relationships: the same people met in a number of different roles – neighbour, relative, friend.[26] This was very uncommon among architects.

A final difference lies in the interconnection of friendship networks, and necessarily follows from the features of the two communities already described. Railwaymen's colleague friends were much more likely to know and be friendly with each other than were the architects'.

26   Some of the railwaymen came from families in which, as they would put it, 'Railways are in the blood'. Forty-one (41.18) per cent of the railwaymen had fathers who were, or still are, railwaymen. (Only 1.92 per cent of the architects had fathers in the profession.) Furthermore, 35.29 per cent of the railwaymen had grandfathers who had been railwaymen; and 82.35 per cent claimed that they had one or more other relatives who had once been, or still were, on the railways.

6
Conclusions and summary

In this book an attempt has been made to bring some order and coherence into discussions of occupational communities. In Chapter 2 a model of the determinants and component elements of occupational communities was presented. This model, and the suggested classification of types of occupational communities, were culled from a thorough overview of the literature on this subject. The following chapters presented an empirical discussion of occupational communities. Chapter 3 dealt with the communities of policemen, jazz musicians, trawlermen and ship-builders; Chapters 4 and 5 presented data on the occupational communities of architects and railwaymen.

The empirical investigations reported in Chapters 4 and 5 were carried out in order to obtain answers to a number of key questions: are the two 'putative' occupational communities which were investigated occupational communities according to the definition given in Chapter 2? Do they differ according to the 'local'/'cosmopolitan' distinction spelt out earlier? If the two 'putative' occupational communities *are* communities so defined, then are they characterised by any of the determinants (involvement in work tasks and skills, marginality and inclusive factors)?

The data presented have supplied answers to these questions. There is no need to restate in detail the conclusions and arguments contained in the two preceding chapters; however some brief summary is appropriate. First it is important to stress that while these data are certainly not adequate to verify satisfactorily the hypotheses outlined earlier, they do certainly suggest that this model will be useful in further investigations of the relationship between work and leisure activities, interests and relations.

Chapter 4 presented data on those factors which, it had previously been suggested, are determinants of occupational communities in that, on the one hand, they motivate men to associate with their work colleagues, carry work activities and interests in their leisure lives and so on, and on the other, that they restrict men's out-of-work freedom. It was argued that both these sorts of factors are causally important, and that the second restrictive type is particularly significant in affecting the pattern of preferential association

114

involved in a particular occupational community (i.e. whether it is local or cosmopolitan.)

Members of both samples display a marked involvement in their work skills and tasks, an involvement which, it has been argued, operates to motivate them to associate with their colleagues and so on. Furthermore both groups were subject to one other sort of determinant. The architects' occupational community was to some extent the consequence of the fact that they shared, as architects, a professional culture which they picked up during their training period. Railwaymen were affected, in their choice of friends and leisure activities, by the restrictive effects of shift work.

Specifically these data show that the majority of both occupational samples see themselves in terms of their occupational role, and that this self-image carries certain conceptions about the people involved: they are felt to be of a particular type. Two-thirds of the architects and 96 per cent of the railwaymen made some sort of occupational identification, and further questioning revealed they shared values and attitudes with other members of their occupation. Finally the data set out in the preceeding chapters reveal that respondents from both samples have a remarkably high number of friends from their occupation, and what's more that they carry work-based interests and activities into their leisure lives.

In short, none of the data presented in the previous two chapters is *inconsistent* with the hypotheses outlined earlier. And the suggestion that the occupational communities can be of two broad types has been substantiated.

The railwaymen's occupational community is characteristically working-class, indeed it is typical of what Lockwood has called 'proletarian traditionalism He writes:

'Workmates are normally leisure-time companions, often neighbours, and not infrequently kinsmen. The existence of such closely-knit cliques of friends, workmates, neighbours and relatives is the hall mark of the traditional working class community. The values expressed through these social networks emphasise mutual aid in everyday life and the obligation to join in the gregarious pattern of leisure, which itself demands the expenditure of time, money and energy in a public and present-oriented conviviality and eschews individual striving "to be different".'[1]

The architects' occupational community, on the other hand, differs in a number of ways from the railwaymen's. Most important, it is based on the

---

1   Lockwood, 'Sources of Variation', p. 251.

occupation or profession *as a whole* rather than on a particular local or departmental group within it. Also of course it is partly the result of shared socialisation and professional training. The architect, like the doctor and the priest (though to a lesser degree), finds that

> 'His occupational role is comprehensive and the implication is that membership of the occupational group confers an acceptable and comprehensive life-style. For such occupations the broader aspects of a socialisation process and educational framework, which not only closely controls selection but also provides training in terms of a general tradition, is clearly particularly appropriate.'[2]

However, despite these differences the main argument of this book has been that there remain significant *similarities* between the two occupational communities; similarities which make it possible and fruitful to consider them — and other communities of this sort — in terms of three component elements and three sorts of determinants.[3]

One point that has not received much attention so far is the distinctiveness of the sorts of work/leisure relationship manifested by members of the two occupational communities. It has been implicit throughout much of the preceding argument that the close interlinking of work and leisure displayed by the architects and railwaymen which has been discussed in the previous chapters is by no means usual in modern industrial societies. Recent research on the work attitudes and behaviour of the so-called 'affluent' worker presents a useful and distinctive comparison. Furthermore this research also suggests that there is a causal link between men's attitudes towards work (essentially this means the extent of their involvement in it), and the sorts of work/leisure relationships they display.

For one thing, it is clear that for those involved in the occupational communities described in the preceding chapters work is very much a central life interest. Dubin has suggested that various areas of work activity may be differently valued by those involved.[4] For some, work is an area of activity that has little if any emotional centrality; as we have seen quite the opposite is true of those involved in occupational communities. Members of occupational

---

2   Jackson, 'Professions and Professionalisation', p. 6.

3   This is an aspect of one of the underlying points of this book: rather than studying occupations in terms of current, accepted categories and classifications — themselves to a great extent, the result of the propaganda of the occupations and the power they can mobilise — their real, functioning similarities should be examined.

4   R. Dubin, 'Industrial Workers' Worlds: A Study of the Central Life Interests of Industrial Workers', *Social Problems*, vol. 4, 1956, pp. 131—42.

communities, it has been argued, are strongly emotionally involved in their work skills and tasks. Involvement refers to: 'the cathectic-evaluative orientation of an actor characterized in terms of intensity and direction'.[5]

As such, involvement means the degree of emotional importance which is attached to an object, activity, relationship or person, *and* to its positive or negative character. Turner has usefully noted that members of work organisations may be differently involved in various aspects of their work at the same time; they can be strongly and positively involved in the organisation as a whole.[6] Something of this sort characterises the architects' and railwaymen's attitudes towards their work and their jobs.

There is considerable evidence that workers in many industries are not involved in their work or their jobs, except, possibly, in a negative sense. For many, the only meaning of work is the money it brings; such workers have what has been called an 'instrumental' orientation towards their work, in that: 'the work situation is defined almost exclusively as a means to an end — that is, almost solely in terms of the economic rewards it offers.'[7]

Goldthorpe *et al.*[8] have found that this sort of instrumentality is particularly typical of workers in assembly-line plants. And there has been some debate as to whether these attitudes are the result of workers' adjusting their wants and expectations in the light of the reality they are faced with (which offers them no opportunity for any other sort of reward but money); or whether they have some sort of previous orientation which guides their choice of work place. Argyris argues in terms of adjustment: 'What has happened to the employees? ... in an attempt to adapt to a world that ideally prefers that they behave like infants, they have finally capitulated and have adapted by becoming apathetic, indifferent, non-involved and so forth.'[9]

But Goldthorpe and his co-authors argue that these attitudes to work have some independent status. They can be seen not as the result of participation in some particular work organisation, but as orientations which predate any particular work experience, and which guide a man to seek out the sort of

5   Etzioni, *A Comparative Analysis,* p. 9.

6   A.N. Turner, 'Foreman, Job and Company', *Human Relations,* vol. 10, 1957, pp. 99–112.

7   G.K. Ingham, 'Organisational Size, Orientation to Work and Industrial Behaviour', *Sociology,* vol. 1, 1967, pp. 239–59, p. 248.

8   Goldthorpe *et al., The Affluent Worker.*

9   Chris Argyris, 'The Organisation: What Makes it Healthy?', *Harvard Business Review,* vol. 36, 1968, pp. 107–16, pp. 109 and 111. See also Argyris, *The Applicability of Organisational Sociology,* chapter 4, and for other views John Child (ed.), *Man and Organisation* (London, Allen and Unwin, 1973).

work which maximises the reward he wants. However this does not mean that these workers are unaware of the deprivations and frustrations to which they are subject; rather that on balance, they are apparently prepared to tolerate them in exchange for other benefits.

Besides offering a remarkable contrast to the sorts of work attitudes displayed by members of occupational communities, the studies discussed above, and particularly the 'affluent worker' study, reveal the very opposite sort of work/leisure relationship to that displayed by people in occupational communities.

It is by no means common for men to have friends from their occupation. Some workers attempt to 'insulate' their non-work lives from any work influence. Goldthorpe *et al.* found that the preponderance of men in their sample neither had relationships of any depth with their work-mates, nor were concerned about having any such relationship. Goldthorpe writes: 'taking the sample as a whole, only around one in four of our affluent workers could be said to have a "close friend" among his mates in the sense of someone with whom he would actually plan to meet for out-of-work social activities.'[10]

These workers are not interested in establishing relationships with their work-mates, rather they wish to demarcate rigidly between the two worlds, and it is the world outside work which is the one that matters.

It must be clear from this book that the determinants and components of occupational communities are closely linked. Men who associate with their work colleagues and who share attitudes, values and interests with them are likely to see their work in terms of these attitudes and values. The architects and railwaymen valued their work because it offered them opportunities to employ skills and techniques they prized, and they saw themselves as certain sorts of people because of their work and the skills and orientations it demanded. And they were proud of these identifications. However, while there is a close connection between participation in an occupational community and involvement in work, it is argued that involvement is a *cause* of men choosing their friends from work, not a *product* of this association.

Why does involvement have such an important effect on men's behaviour and attitudes to work, and why does it encourage them to carry work

10   Goldthorpe *et al., The Affluent Worker,* p. 56. Other writers have also commented on the separation of work and leisure. Zweig, in his study *The Worker in an Affluent Society,* shows that work-based friendships are comparatively rare among the sample of workers with which he was concerned. He writes: 'The contacts with work-mates apart from work seemed to be sporadic. The majority of workers would subscribe to the saying which I often heard that "mates are not pals".' (F. Zweig, *The Worker in an Affluent Society* (London, Heinemann, 1961), p. 117.)

activities, interests and relationships outside work? The simple answer to this is that involvement implies men's attitudes, and feelings for, certain characteristics of an activity they have in common. A theme of basic importance underlying the skills and techniques men value, is that of meaningfulness. When men are involved in their work (or anything for that matter) they define it as having importance and significance.

Involvement implies a particular relationship between work and the larger society. In some cases the larger society can be taken to mean society as a whole; at other times it might be a local class or regional community; but the point remains that because certain significant others grant a particular meaning to a certain activity, men in certain lines of work consider their participation in a work role is an important and meaningful aspect of their own identity; i.e. they are involved. Since, therefore, involvement means that men consider a particular activity or relationship is significant for their view of themselves, it is not surprising that they are keen to associate with others who are similarly involved, and to carry their interest in the activity into their leisure-time activity. For members of occupational communities, if not for all workers in industrial societies, work is 'one of the things by which he is judged, and certainly one of the significant things by which he judges himself'.[11] Thus involvement can be seen as the opposite of alienation, as defined by Faunce, who writes that it occurs when 'the criteria we use to evaluate ourselves are different from the criteria used by others in evaluating us'.[12]

However, it is not the case that any sort of work can be seen as important, valuable, manly, dangerous, etc. The work tasks themselves, seen objectively and detachedly, are most important, as is the sort of definitions of these activities current with the larger society. There are a number of criteria current within various groups which are used to evaluate work and work tasks. There is no reason to suppose societal consensus on this. As Parkin has remarked, the apparent agreement within all strata of society on the status ranking of occupations may well reflect awareness, on the part of those in the working class, of the occupational ranking used by middle-class people, rather than their own evaluations and attitudes.[13]

11 Everett C. Hughes, 'Work and the Self', in J. Rohrer and M. Sherif (ed.), *Social Psychology at the Crossroads* (New York, Harper and Row, 1951), p. 313. Quoted in Faunce, *Problems of an Industrial Society*, p. 116.

12 Faunce, *Problems of an Industrial Society*, p. 94.

13 Frank Parkin, *Class Inequality and Political Order* (London, MacGibbon and Kee, 1971), p. 41.

It is being suggested then, that involvement in work tasks and skills is the essential determinant of occupational communities and that involvement itself is an attitude towards certain aspects of work, viewed objectively, which are defined as valuable, important or in some other sense meaningful by some if not all members of society. For example, there is presumably a high degree of agreement about the value and importance of medicine (indeed Krause has suggested that a profession can be defined in terms of its 'power to determine its place and function in the community, its relation to the work of other occupations, and its mode of everyday operation'.[14] But the definition and evaluation of other occupations vary; some groups within society might assess an occupation in terms described above, while others might not see it as in any way distinctive. Also there is no reason to suppose that people's attitudes towards and evaluation of occupations are consistent and homogeneous; some ambivalence is quite likely.

While an occupational community obviously perpetuates and transmits work attitudes, as the previous chapters have shown, involvement is, finally, based on work which is defined and evaluated in certain ways by people generally, so that there is a 'real' basis for it being regarded as important and valuable. This means that certain aspects of work and work tasks must be seen as important, valuable and meaningful by people other than members of the occupation itself. (This does not mean that the job as a whole need be valued, but that *some* characteristics of it, or activities that it involves, must be so defined.) When the work loses these 'involvement-arousing' characteristics, then, *over time*, changes will take place in the work-based attitudes and relationships of the men concerned. This is happening with the railwaymen.

Needless to say this will be a bitter personal disappointment to those concerned.

The most important 'involvement-arousing' factors seem to be:

1. Danger. It seems, *a priori,* unlikely that work which involves danger to life or limb will not be seen as significant, meaningful, and probably manly, by those who do it and by outsiders.

2. Skilled work, in that the work requires the application of knowledge and expertise, technical or manual, and that it is relatively free from interference or supervision.

3. Work that takes place under extreme conditions of some sort, or is defined as unusual. For example very arduous work, or work that exposes men to extreme discomfort.

14   Krause, *The Sociology of Occupations,* pp. 47–8.

4. Work that is considered important in some sense. Often this will mean that the work is in some way concerned with core societal values and events. The idea of 'social value' has two elements: the notion that the work is important, and the difficulty of replacing the personnel who do it. Some work is functionally important, but those who do it derive little bargaining power from this because the job requires no training and its personnel can be readily replaced. One of the features of professions, in this context, is that they manage to disseminate their own view of the importance, necessity and sacredness of their work outside the occupation[15] and then use this accepted definition of the work as a justification for organising and controlling lengthy periods of training and socialisation. These then serve to increase the importance of the occupation by making its practitioners irreplaceable, at least in the short term.

Work tasks and activities, while important as the basis of involvement, are by no means the only important aspects of work. In the case of the railwaymen in particular, it is clear that relationships with the employer also have considerable significance. Historically relationships between railwaymen and their employer had three characteristics: the job was secure; promotion, though extremely slow, was more or less predictable; and the railwaymen's skills were untransferable. These factors, the first two of which have changed in recent years, undoubtedly affected railwaymen's marked feelings of group solidarity, and their willingness to relate to their work-mates. Because of conditions within their industry railwaymen did not develop the sort of individualism which characterises members of other occupations: there was very little competition between the railwaymen for promotion, and, because of the lack of transferability, they were unwilling to leave the railways. Consequently they could not avoid, even if they had wanted to, relationships with their work-mates.[16]

Chapter 5 presented data on the value systems of the two occupational communities. It is clear that these involve very similar elements, more or less developed and explicit. These value systems comprise statements of the importance and utility of the occupational tasks. Both contain a view of the essential work tasks of members of the occupation, and the skills, attitudes, orientations and disciplines that are necessary. Both emphasise the importance of the work tasks, by focussing on the rarity of the attitudes, skills, etc., that

15   See Dibble, 'Occupations and Ideologies'.

16   For a fuller discussion of the origins of individualism among navvies, see A.J.M. Sykes, 'Navvies: Their Work Attitudes', *Sociology*, vol. 3, 1969, pp. 21–36, and 'Navvies: Their Social Relations', *Sociology*, vol. 3, pp. 157–73.

are necessary, the importance of independence and the social function of the occupation. No doubt there are other elements involved, and these could be usefully explored, but this must await further research.

These occupational value systems stem from the shared problems, difficulties and techniques faced by members of occupations; but they also serve to formulate and maintain a system of definitions and interpretations of these problems and the shared interests of members of the occupation. It is interesting that, although neither of the two occupations described in this book appears to have developed anything like coherent systematic political cultures, or class consciousness, radical class consciousness does seem to be based very frequently on occupational groups: it develops as a response to deterioration in conditions and circumstances, which is then generalised to other groups. This is not to suggest that each occupation constitutes a separate class, but that class is a way of categorising the sorts of experiences men are exposed to because of their place in the economic order. As Thompson puts it:

> 'class happens when some men, as a result of common experiences (inherited or shared), feel and articulate the identity of their interests as between themselves, and as against other men whose interests are different from (and usually opposed to) theirs. The class experience is largely determined by the productive relations into which men are born — or enter involuntarily. Class-consciousness is the way in which these experiences are handled in cultural terms: embodied in traditions, value-systems, ideas, and institutional forms.'[17]

This is not to deny the validity of the working-class/middle-class distinction. Certainly there is evidence that this is a useful way of categorising real differences in life chances, and market and work situations. However, *it is* to suggest that the usual argument in terms of working-class and middle-class *cultures* can be overstated. Empirical investigation reveals a number of differences in culture between working-class occupations. Occupation is an important factor in the development and transmission of a traditional, established or professional value system which projects the interests of an occupation and argues either for the improvement of the position of the occupation, or the maintenance of the *status quo*. It is also a factor in the development of new, possibly radical perspectives to fill the gap between what is 'normal', expected and 'necessary' for the proper execution of work tasks, and new conditions. This new perspective is the result of the old one plus new circumstances, and

17   E.P. Thompson, *The Making of the English Working Class* (Harmondsworth, Penguin, 1968), pp. 9–10.

it must be seen in terms of the history of the occupation and the desires, now unrealised, of members of the occupation, for certain levels of security, status opportunities for advancement, opportunities to use skills, etc.[18]

However, radical ideologies are the result of previous ideologies — their unsuitability and inappropriateness — and are limited and constrained by these old ideologies. Men do not give up everything they believe because some of it no longer fits, and the way they reject the old, and their receptivity to new beliefs will be affected by the way they used to see things. This is particularly true of the railwaymen in the sample who, because of the value they placed on service, responsibility, dedication, etc. (see Chapter 5), regarded the changes in their work with personal disappointment and bitterness, but were unwilling, at the time of the study, to adopt militant union tactics. Their view of the world was one of disappointment at their unappreciated loyalty.

It is only possible to understand the position, experiences and behaviour of members of the two occupational samples described in this book by considering these things in a historical perspective, by considering the ability, or inability, of members of the two occupations to check or control these changes which have taken or are taking place, and, underlying these changes, the sorts of expectations and values that the men concerned hold about their work; expectations, which, while once more or less accurate reflections of work reality, may be increasingly inappropriate. To quote Goldthorpe *et al.*, whose study explicitly focusses on the actual nature of workers' socially derived work expectations: 'in seeking to explain and to understand attitudes, behaviour and social relationships within a particular work situation, analysis will more usefully begin with the orientations to work which are found to prevail, rather

18   It is a further theme of this book that the sociology of occupations is a very important branch of sociological thought, both theoretically and substantively. The study of occupations as communities or groups is important for the way in which it

> 'stresses one particular aspect, namely the way in which patterns of social relationships are developed, perpetuated and discontinued between networks of persons participating in similar activities in the division of labour. It also implies examining the ways in which such networks of persons set about identifying and pursuing what they consider to be their collective occupational interests.' (C. Turner and M.N. Hodge, 'Occupations and Professions', in Jackson, *Professions,* pp. 17–50, p. 35.)

than with quite general assumptions about the needs which all workers have.'[19]

Occupational Communities?

How far can the phenomena described in this book be regarded as occupational *communities?* It might be argued that because of the differences between the two occupations it is confusing to consider both of them as communities. Alternatively it might be suggested that the architects' case can hardly be considered as bona-fide community since it lacks the important defining characteristic of geographical propinquity.

As previously mentioned, Nisbet has noted that the concept 'community' was of central importance when sociology was emerging as a separate discipline. It was used to describe those relationships and experiences, and the way in which they were patterned and inter-related, which the early sociologists considered were being radically disrupted by the twin processes of industrial and political change. When used by the early sociologists the term 'community' referred to, pinpointed and described the break-up of the old order. As such, this concept, which above all others emphasises stability and equilibrium if not changelessness, is itself a product of a changing social order, and indeed only makes sense in conjuction with its opposite, however this is described and evaluated. Interest in community developed out of an attempt to explain and understand its disruption.

Nisbet summaries this classic view of community thus:

'The . . . word encompasses all forms of relationship which are characterized by a high degree of personal intimacy, emotional depth, moral commitment, social cohesion, and continuity in time. Community is founded on man conceived in his wholeness rather than in one or another of the roles, taken separately, that he may hold in a social order.'[20]

---

19   Goldthorpe *et al., The Affluent Worker,* p. 179. The notion 'orientations to work' is by no means without problems. For one thing, the answers people give to questions involve some choice from among a relatively limited repertoire of culturally available responses. Thus different situations (one of which is the interview situation) will produce different sorts of response. It has also been argued that some degree of work socialisation is important. For a discussion of these and other difficulties see Richard Brown, 'Sources of Objectives in Work and Employment', and W.W. Danniel, 'Understanding Employee Behaviour in its Context: Illustrations from Productivity Bargaining', in Child, *Man and Organization,* pp. 17—38 and 39—63.

20   Nisbet, *The Sociological Tradition,* p. 47.

That community means men relate to each other wholly, rather than in a specific role, is basic to most definitions of it. However, because of its importance it is not surprising to learn that there is as little sociological agreement on the meaning of this term as any other. Hillyer collected together ninety-four different definitions, and despite certain areas of agreement within these definitions, recurring ambiguities remain. It is because of these that Stacey has recently remarked: 'It is doubtful whether the concept "community" refers to a useful abstraction. Certainly confusion continues to reign over the use of the term.'[21]

The main confusion, as Stacey notes, is that between community as a *geographical entity* and community as a *type of relationship*. Sometimes these are referred to, respectively, as 'a community', and 'Community'. Of course, ideally, these two converge, and one finds a particular geographical area characterised by a distinctive network of interlocking relationships so that people meet and relate to each other in a number of roles. This is the sort of definition Frankenberg uses:

'In face-to-face communities each individual is related to every other individual in his total network in several different ways. In extreme case a man's father is also his teacher, his religious leader and his employer. A shopkeeper in the village is also a relative of many of his customers and a chapel deacon.'[22]

Many writers have used the term to refer to this sort of overlapping of interlocked relationships and geographical area.

However, because of concern for the sorts of relationship characteristic of communities of this type, recent writers have used the term 'community' to refer to particular sorts of inter-relationships and the feelings of solidarity and communality associated with them. Community in this sense is used to refer to an 'integrated system of social life' which does not necessarily occur within a limited geographical area. This use of community sometimes refers to the sorts of relationships that occur — i.e. that people interact in many roles — or to a community of interest and values — as Mack and Merriam put it: 'We use community here not to denote a group with a geographical locus, but in the sense of a community of interest; what is implied by the word is that the people described here share a set of norms.'[23]

21   Margaret Stacey, 'The Myth of Community Studies', *British Journal of Sociology*, vol. 20, no. 2, June 1969, pp. 134–48, p. 134.

22   Ronald Frankenberg, *Communities in Britain: Social Life in Town and Country* (Harmondsworth, Penguin, 1966), p. 17.

23   Mack and Merriam, 'The Jazz Community', p. 211.

This normative use is employed by Goode, who argues that professions are communities because members are, among other things, bound to each other a by common sense of identity and by a common value system.

However, if community is used without any necessary reference to geographical location two points follow: first, that just as a community need not exist within a limited area, so people who live within a limited area need not constitute a community; secondly, without the geographical factor, the degree to which institutions are integrated and the same people relate to each other in a number of roles is clearly likely to be less. It was found that the railwaymen related to each other in more roles (relative, friend, neighbour and workmate) than the architects; and this follows from the fact that the railwaymen worked and lived together. When a community lacks any geographical limitation it is to be expected that members will interact in fewer roles.

It comes as no surprise to learn that sociologists use and define the concept 'community' differently. As has been argued, it was, and to a lesser extent still is, central to the sorts of issues that sociology was originally developed to describe and explain, and, what's more, is closely related to the sorts of moral concerns of the founding fathers of sociology. The disagreement is far more important and substantial than a mere argument over the use of words; it reflects, as does any discussion of concepts, theoretical issues and debates, however implicit and unformulated these may be. Consequently, to argue that a particular way of using a concept is justified does not mean that it is established and respectable; the important thing is to show that by using the concept in this way one is drawing attention to certain sorts of sociologically significant relationships.

The difficulty is, of course, that however one might like to define a concept or the meaning of a word, words carry residual meanings and associations, which is why it is possible to sympathise with those who wish to reject any further use of the concept 'community'. This difficulty is particularly acute in this case because the original meaning of the term, as used by the founding fathers, is less appropriate when describing the sorts of relationships current within industrial societies; even the most 'community-like' are still far removed from the sorts of situations that Tonnies, Durkheim, etc., were considering when they referred to Gemeinschaft society, or mechanical solidarity.

However, describing the two communities discussed in this book as occupational communities can be justified in a number of ways. First, even within the history of the concept 'community' there is justification for referring to both occupational samples as occupational communities. The important aspects of the two samples are: that members associated with and related to each other in more than one role, and that the roles within which they interacted were of importance to them; that they shared a body of interests and values. Of course there is hardly any need to justify the use of the term in the railwaymen's case since they interact in many roles and live within the same area.

Secondly, it is the contention of this book that the phenomena described constitute an important, distinctive and by no means residual type of work/ leisure relationship; a relationship which is not only important in its own right but which is also significant for the way in which it differs from other sorts of relationships between men's work and leisure. And to refer to this as an occupational community highlights the distinctive quality of this relation- ship — the remarkable intermingling of work and non-work activities, relation- ships, values, interests and identities. The concept 'occupational community' is not merely some sort of classificatory heading, a new category in a catalogue of social taxonomy. There is little to be gained from arguments as to whether a particular occupation is or is not an occupational community. Instead it is a way of looking at and analysing the relationship between work and leisure, certain features of work activities and organisation and the socially based meaning that is attached to them — either nationally, or locally — and the ways in which they impinge on, and restrict, men's non-work activities and relationships. Thus it could be argued that *all* occupations that are not mere classificatory headings involve, to some extent, some of the characteristics of an occupational community as described.

Furthermore it is probably more fruitful to consider the concept 'occu- pational community' in terms of degree rather than in terms of its presence or absence. In this way one's attention is drawn to interesting and significant aspects of occupations as collectivities, rather than as mere census categories. At the same time if the researcher considers the extent to which communities display the various community characteristics he is forced to examine the ways in which the term 'occupation' is employed by those who are being researched, rather than by those who are carrying out the research. There is a definite tendency for the idea of 'occupation' — when used to refer to a collectivity rather than a census category — to be used very loosely, a 'you- know-what-I-mean' concept, defined differently by the sociologist and an

127

occupation.[24] This confusion between sociological and lay uses of the concept is particularly unfortunate when the sociologist is actually interested in discovering when people see themselves as members of an occupation, i.e. when they actually employ the concept 'occupation' as a way of describing certain significant groupings and memberships. And it is when an occupation is seen as a collectivity, as a significant membership category by those concerned, that the concept 'occupational community' (seen in terms of degree of 'community') as set out in this book is well suited to describe it. Thus the idea of occupational community forces one back to investigate what occurs when persons see themselves in terms of their membership of an occupation − as *they* define it − and the conditions under which this definition and identification come about.

Occupational community, it is being argued, can usefully be employed not in some nostalgic search for residual geographical working-class occupational communities, but as a way of analysing and discussing a particular sort of work/leisure link which involves persons in defining themselves in terms of their membership of an occupation − as they see it − and the patterns of relationship, solidarity and exclusion that follow. It is interesting that such a perspective on the concept 'occupational community' is in line with earlier sources of interest which derived from a concern for analysing the possible links between patterns of work/community relationship and the development of class or radical consciousness. These early typologies and hypotheses on the nature of such relationships have in many cases been overtaken by more recent research (which has pointed out the complexity of 'work situations' and the diversity and variability of images of society); in particular the view

24   Warnings about this sort of short-circuiting have been given by Harvey Sacks, among others. He writes:

> 'Sociologists frequently treat some categorization that Members have done as providing the sociologist with materials that are descriptive in the sense that such materials may then be used − as they stand − for further sociological investigation. Alternatively, sociologists themselves frequently use Members' categorization devices to categorize Members as one step in doing sociological inquiries. In both cases the presumptive warrant for this usage is or would seem to be that the demonstrable correctness of the categorization may properly be established by some such procedure as looking to see whether the object (person) so categorized, was properly categorized, i.e. by observing, for example, that the Member categorized as "negro" is a negro.'

Sacks goes on to warn that such a presumptive warrant is inadequate. As the ethnomethodologists see it, a great deal of confusion is caused, in sociology, by the confusion of lay and sociological uses of definitions. (Harvey Sacks, 'An Initial Investigation of the Usability of Conversational Data for Doing Sociology', in David Sudnow (ed.), *Studies in Social Interaction* (New York, Free Press, 1972), p. 33.)

that a working-class occupational community produces a class-conscious view of the world in its members is now felt to be suspect. It is of course true that membership of an occupational community will bring a strong sense of identity, of solidarity with colleagues (as this term is employed by members) and of separateness from those outside the occupation. But such an awareness (often revealed in discussions with the architects and railwaymen by such comments as 'We're a race apart') is an entirely different thing from a class-conscious view of the world. Indeed the them/us view could, hypothetically, lead to a strongly reactionary political line.

Nevertheless, although the sort of work/leisure relationship described here and elsewhere as an occupational community is no longer considered a necessary source of radical images of society, it has been argued in this book that the concept can still be usefully employed in investigating people's definitions, perceptions and images of themselves within the division of labour. Thus the concept is still basically concerned with images, definitions and assessments in as far as these derive from and are used to categorise and evaluate the nature of work and the meaning of occupation and colleagueship.

Bibliography

Abrams, M. (1964) 'Architects', an *Observer* Survey.

Albrow, M. (1970) *Bureaucracy,* London, Macmillan.

Argyris, Chris (1968) 'The Organisation: What Makes it Healthy?', *Harvard Business Review,* 36, pp. 107–16.

Argyris, Chris (1972) *The Applicability of Organizational Sociology,* Cambridge University Press.

Banton, M. (1964) *The Policeman in the Community,* London, Tavistock Publications.

Becker, H.S. and Carper, J.W. (1956) 'Elements of Identification with an Occupation', *American Sociological Review,* 21, pp. 341–8.

Becker, H.S. and Strauss, A.L. (1956) 'Careers, Personality and Adult Socialisation', *American Journal of Sociology,* vol. 62, pp. 253–63.

Becker, H.S. (1963) *Outsiders,* New York, Free Press.

Becker, H.S. (1964) 'Personal Change in Adult Life', *Sociometry,* pp. 40–53.

Berger, P.L. and Luckmann, T. (1969) *The Social Construction of Reality,* London, Allen Lane.

Blakelock, E. (1960) 'New Look at Old Leisure', *Administrative Science Quarterly,* vol. 4, pp. 446–67.

Blauner R. (1964) *Alienation and Freedom,* University of Chicago Press.

Blum, F.H. (1963) *Towards a Democratic Work Process,* New York, Harper and Row.

Bohannon, Paul (1964) 'Conscience Collective and Culture', in Wolff, Kurt H. (ed.), *Essay on Sociology and Philosophy by Emile Durkheim et al.* New York, Harper and Row, pp. 77–96.

Bonnar, Robert (1969) 'Negotiating at the Top', in Fraser, Ronald (ed.), *Work Volume 2: Twenty Personal Accounts,* Harmondsworth, Penguin, pp. 330–45.

Brennan, T., Cooney, E.W. and Pollins, H. (1954) *Social Change in South West Wales,* London, Watts.

Brown, Richard and Brennen, Peter (1970) 'Social Relations and Social Perspectives Amongst Shipbuilding Workers', Part I, *Sociology,* vol. 4, pp. 71–84.

Brown, Richard and Brennen, Peter (1970) 'Social Relations and Social Perspectives Amongst Shipbuilding Workers', Part II, *Sociology,* vol. 4, pp. 197–211.

Brown, Richard (1973) 'Sources of Objectives in Work and Employment', in Child, John (ed.), *Man and Organization,* London, Allen and Unwin, pp. 17–38.

Cain, Maureen (1971) 'On the Beat: Interactions and Relations in Rural and Urban Police Forces', in Cohen, Stan (ed.), *Images of Deviance,* Harmondsworth, Penguin, pp. 62–97.

Cameron, William B. (1954) 'Sociological Notes on the Jam Session', *Social Forces,* vol. 33, pp. 177–82.

Cannon, I.C. (1967) 'Ideology and Occupational Community: A Study of Compositors', *Sociology,* vol. 1, pp. 160–87.

130

Carr-Saunders, A.M. and Wilson, P.A. (1933) *The Professions,* Oxford University Press.

Child, John (ed.) (1973) *Man and Organization,* London, Allen and Unwin.

Chinoy, E. (1953) *Automobile Workers and the American Dream,* New York, Doubleday.

Cotgrove, Stephen and Box, Steven (1970) *Science Industry and Society,* London, Allen and Unwin.

Cottrell, W.F. (1940) *The Railroader,* Stanford University Press.

Daniel, W.W. (1973) 'Understanding Employee Behaviour in its Context: Illustrations from Productivity Bargaining', in Child, John (ed.), *Man and Organization,* London, Allen and Unwin, pp. 39–63.

Dawe, Alan (1970) 'The Two Sociologies', *British Journal of Sociology,* vol. 21, no. 2, pp. 207–18.

Denzin, N.K. (1968) 'Pharmacy – Incomplete Professionalisation', *Social Forces,* vol. 46, no. 3, p. 376.

Dibble, Vernon (1962) 'Occupations and Ideologies', *American Journal of Sociology,* vol. 68, pp. 229–41.

Dubin, R. (1956) 'Industrial Workers' Worlds: A Study of the Central Life Interests of Industrial Workers', *Social Problems,* 4, pp. 131–42.

Durkheim, Emile (1951) *Suicide: A Study in Sociology,* translated by Spaulding, John A. and Simpson, George, edited with an introduction by Simpson, George, New York, Free Press.

Durkheim, Emile (1957) *Professional Ethics and Civic Morals,* translated by Brookfield, Cornelia, London, Routledge and Kegan Paul.

Durkheim, Emile (1962) *Socialism,* edited with an introduction by Gouldner, Alvin, New York, Collier Books and Antioch Press.

Eldridge, J.E.T. (1968) 'The Demarcation Dispute in the Shipbuilding Industry', in Eldridge, J.E.T., *Industrial Disputes,* London, Routledge and Kegan Paul, pp. 91–154.

Etzioni, A. (1961) *A Comparative Analysis of Complex Organisations,* New York, Free Press.

Faunce, William A. (1968) *Problems of an Industrial Society,* New York, McGraw-Hill.

Feuer, L. (1962) 'What is Alienation? The Career of a Concept', *New Politics,* vol. 1, no. 3, pp. 116–34.

Frankenberg, Ronald (1966) *Communities in Britain: Social Life in Town and Country,* Harmondsworth, Penguin.

Fraser, Ronald (ed.) (1969) *Work Volume 2: Twenty Personal Accounts,* Harmondsworth, Penguin.

Freund, J. (1968) *The Sociology of Max Weber,* London, Allen Lane.

Geertz, Clifford (1964) 'Ideology as a Cultural System', in Apter, David (ed.), *Ideology and Discontent,* New York, Free Press, pp. 47–76.

Gerstl, J.E. (1961) 'Determinants of Occupational Community in High Status Occupations', *Sociology Quarterly,* vol. 2, pp. 37–48.

Gerth, H.H. and Mills, C.W. (1954) *Character and Social Structure,* London, Routledge and Kegan Paul.

Goffman, E. (1959) *The Presentation of Self in Everyday Life,* New York, Doubleday.

Goffman, E. (1961) *Asylums,* New York, Doubleday.

Goffman, E. (1961) *Encounters: Two Studies in the Sociology of Interaction,* New York, Bobbs-Merrill.

Goffman, E. (1969) *Where the Action Is,* London, Allen Lane.

Goffman, E. (1969) 'Role Distance', in Goffman, E., *Where the Action Is,* London, Allen Lane, pp. 37–103.

Goldthorpe, John H., Lockwood, David, Bechhofer, Frank and Platt, Jennifer (1968) *The Affluent Worker: Industrial Attitudes and Behaviour,* Cambridge University Press.

Goode, W.J. (1957) 'Community within a Community: The Professions', *American Sociological Review,* vol. 22, pp. 194–200.

Gotch, Christopher (1969) 'The Architect', in Fraser, Ronald (ed.), *Work Volume 2: Twenty Personal Accounts,* Harmondsworth, Penguin, pp. 147–64.

Gouldner, A.W. (1957) 'Cosmopolitans and Locals: Towards an Analysis of Latent Social Roles', *Administrative Science Quarterly,* vol. 2, pp. 281–306.

Gouldner, H.P. (1960) 'Dimensions of Organisational Commitment', *Administrative Science Quarterly,* vol. 4, pp. 468–90.

Griff, M. (1960) 'The Commercial Artist. A Study in Changing and Consistent Identities', in Stein, Maurice, Vidich, A.J. and White, David Manning, (ed.), *Identity and Anxiety. Survival of the Person in Mass Society,* New York, Free Press, pp. 219–41.

Gross, N., Mason, W. and McEachern, A.W. (1958) *Explorations in Role Analysis: Studies of the School Superintendency Role,* New York, Wiley.

Harris, Nigel (1971) *Beliefs in Society: The Problems of Ideology,* Harmondsworth, Penguin.

Hindess, Barry (1971) *The Decline of Working Class Politics,* London, MacGibbon and Kee.

Homans, G.C. (1961) *Social Behaviour: Its Elementary Forms,* London, Routledge and Kegan Paul.

Horobin, G.W. (1957) 'Community and Occupation in the Hull Fishing Industry', *British Journal of Sociology,* vol. 8, pp. 343–56.

Hughes, Everett C. (1951) 'Work and the Self', in Rohrer, J. and Sherif, M. (eds.), *Social Psychology at the Crossroads,* New York, Harper and Row, pp. 313–23.

Hughes, Everett C. (1958) *Men and Their Work,* Glencoe, Illinois, Free Press.

Ingham, G.K. (1967) 'Organizational Size, Orientation to Work and Industrial Behaviour', *Sociology,* vol. 1, pp. 239–59.

Ingham, G.K. (1970) *Size of Industrial Organization and Worker Behaviour,* Cambridge University Press.

Jackson, J.A. (1970) 'Profession and Professionalisation – Editorial Introduction', in Jackson, J.A. (ed.), *Professions and Professionalisation,* Cambridge University Press, pp. 1–15.

James, William (1968) 'The Self', in Gordon, Chad and Gergen, Kenneth J. (eds.), *The Self in Social Interaction,* New York, Wiley, pp. 41–9.

Janowitz, M. (1960) *The Professional Soldier,* Glencoe, Illinois, Free Press.

Kaye, Barrington (1960) *The Development of the Architectural Profession in Britain, A Sociological Study,* London, Allen and Unwin.

Kluckhohn, Clyde (1962) 'Values and Value-Orientations in the Theory of Action: An Exploration in Definition and Classification', in Parsons, Talcott and Shils, Edward A. (eds.), *Towards a General Theory of Action: Theoretical Foundations for the Social Sciences,* New York, Harper and Row, pp. 388–433.

Krause, Elliott A. (1971) *The Sociology of Occupations,* Boston, Little, Brown and Company.

Kuhn, M.H. and McPartland, Thomas S. (1954) 'An Empirical Investigation of Self Attitudes', *American Sociological Review,* vol. 19, pp. 68–76.

Lenski, G.E. (1954) 'Status Crystallization: A Non-Vertical Dimension of Social Status', *American Sociological Review,* vol. 19, pp. 405–13.

Lipman, Alan (1960) 'The Architectural Belief System and Social Behaviour', *British Journal of Sociology,* vol. 20, pp. 190–204.

Lipset, S.M., Trow, M.A. and Coleman, J.S. (1956) *Union Democracy: The Internal Politics of the International Typographical Union,* Glencoe, Illinois, Free Press.

Lockwood, D. (1966) 'Sources of Variation in Working Class Images of Society', *Sociological Review,* vol. 14, pp. 249–62.

Mack, R.W. (1956) 'Occupational Determinateness', *Social Forces,* vol. 35, pp. 20–35.

Mack, R.W. and Merriam, A.P. (1960) 'The Jazz Community', *Social Forces,* vol. 35, pp. 211–22.

McLellan, David (1971) *Marx's Grundrisse,* London, Macmillan.

Marcus, P. (1960) 'Expressive and Instrumental Groups: Towards a Theory of Group Structure', *American Sociological Review,* vol. 66, pp. 54–9.

Marx, Karl (1967) *Economic and Philosophical Manuscripts of 1844,* London, Lawrence and Wishart.

Marx, Karl and Engels, Friedrich (1961) From 'The Communist Manifesto', in Bottomore, T.B. and Rubel, M. (eds.), *Karl Marx: Selected Writings in Sociology and Social Philosophy,* Harmondsworth, Penguin, p. 192.

Mead, G.H. (1932) *The Philosophy of the Present,* Chicago, Open Court Publishing Company.

Merton, R.K. (1957) *Social Theory and Social Structure,* New York, Free Press. Reprinted 1962, Glencoe, Illinois, Free Press.

Merton, R.K. Reader, G.G. and Kendall, Patricia L. (eds.), (1957) *The Student Physician,* Harvard University Press.

Meszaros, I. (1970) *Marx's Theory of Alienation,* London, Merlin Press.

Mills, C.W. (1956) *White Collar: The American Middle Classes,* New York, Galaxy.

Morris, T. and Morris, P. (1963) *Pentonville: A Sociological Study of an English Prison,* London, Routledge and Kegan Paul.

Mott, P.E., Mann, F.C., McLoughlin, Q. and Warick, P.P. (1956) *Shift Work: The Social, Psychological and Physical Consequences,* University of Michigan Press.

Nisbet, Robert (1967) *The Sociological Tradition,* London, Heinemann.

Ogden, C.K. and Richards, I.A. (1949) *The Meaning of Meaning,* London, Routledge and Kegan Paul.

Park, R. (1931) 'Human Nature, Attitudes and Mores', in Young, Kimball (ed.), *Social Attitudes,* New York, Holt, pp. 17–45. Quoted in Gordon, C. and Gergen, K.J. (eds.), *The Self in Social Interaction,* New York, Wiley, 1968, p. 94.

Parker, S.R. (1964) 'Type of Work, Friendship Patterns, and Leisure', *Human Relations,* vol. 17, pp. 215–19.

Parkin, Frank (1971) *Class Inequality and Political Order,* London, MacGibbon and Kee.

Polsky, Ned (1971) *Hustlers, Beats and Others,* Harmondsworth, Penguin.

Reissman, L. (1949) 'A Study in Role Conceptions in Bureaucracy', *Social Forces,* vol. 27, pp. 306–31.

Rose, Arnold (1971) 'A Systematic Summary of Symbolic Interaction Theory', in Rose, Arnold (ed.), *Human Behaviour and Social Processes,* London, Routledge and Kegan Paul, pp. 3–19.

Sacks, Harvey (1972) 'An Initial Investigation of the Usability of Conversational Data for Doing Sociology', in Sudnow, David (ed.), *Studies in Social Interaction,* New York, Free Press, pp. 31–74.

Salaman, Graeme (1973) 'Occupations, Community and Consciousness', in Bulmer, M.I.A. (ed.), *Studies in Working Class Imagery,* London, Routledge and Kegan Paul.

Schacht, Richard (1970) *Alienation,* London, Allen and Unwin.

Sherif, M. and Cantril, H. (1947) *The Psychology of Ego-Involvements,* New York, Wiley.

Sherif, M. and Sherif, C.W. (1964) *Reference Groups: Exploration into Conformity and Deviation of Adolescents,* New York, Harper and Row.

Shibutani, T. (1971) 'Reference Groups and Social Control', in Rose, Arnold (ed.), *Human Behaviour and Social Processes,* London, Routledge and Kegan Paul, pp. 128–47.

Simpson, R.L. and Simpson, Idd H. (1959) 'The Psychiatric Attendant, Development of an Occupational Self Image in a Low Status Occupation', *American Sociological Review,* vol. 24, pp. 389–92.

Stacey, Margaret (1969) 'The Myth of Community Studies', *British Journal of Sociology,* vol. 20, no. 2, pp. 134–48.

Strauss, A. (1959) *Mirrors and Masks,* Glencoe, Illinois, Free Press.

Strauss, G. (1962) 'Professionalism and Occupational Associations', *Industrial Relations,* vol. 2, pp. 7–31.

Sykes, A.J.M. (1969) 'Navvies: Their Work Attitudes', *Sociology,* vol. 3, pp. 21–36.

Sykes, A.J.M. (1969) 'Navvies: Their Social Relations', *Sociology,* vol. 3, pp. 157–73.

Thompson, E.P. (1968) *The Making of the English Working Class,* Harmondsworth, Penguin.

Tönnies, F. (1955) *Community and Association,* London, Routledge and Kegan Paul.

Tunstall, J. (1969) *The Fishermen: The Sociology of an Extreme Occupation,* London, MacGibbon and Kee.

Turner, A.N. (1957) 'Foreman, Job and Company', *Human Relations,* vol. 10, pp. 99–112.

Turner, C. and Hodge, M.N. (1970) 'Occupations and Professions', Jackson, J.A. (ed.), *Professions and Professionalisation,* Cambridge University Press, pp. 17–50.

Weber, Max (1961) 'Science as a Vocation', in Gerth, H.H. and Mills, C.W. (eds.), *From Max Weber: Essays in Sociology,* London, Routledge and Kegan Paul, pp. 129–56.

Weber, Max (1961) 'Bureaucracy', in Gerth, H.H. and Mills, C.W. (eds.), *From Max Weber: Essays in Sociology,* London, Routledge and Kegan Paul, pp. 196–244.

Young, J. (1971) 'The Role of the Police as Amplifiers of Deviancy . . .', in Cohen, Stan (ed.), *Images of Deviance,* Harmondsworth, Penguin, pp. 27–61.

Zweig, F. (1961) *The Worker in an Affluent Society,* London, Heinemann.

Index